Mor

A Field Guide to the English Clergy

'Eye-popping tales of lunacy, debauchery and depravity... Butler-Gallie knows whereof he writes, being a curate himself, and he has done a splendid job presenting a smorgasbord of most peculiar parsons.'

Sebastian Shakespeare, *Daily Mail*

'Entertainingly erudite... But it is also a surprisingly profound work... For all its mischief, Butler-Gallie's work of lightly worn erudition is a paean to a great English institution, finely tuned to the temper of its representatives, good, bad and indifferent. We should treasure it more.'

Literary Review

'We have...always kept a special haven for oddballs in the Church of England, as Fergus Butler-Gallie demonstrates in this entertaining compendium... Their foibles cover all bases from absentmindedness to epic drunkenness... I'm glad I read this one. It's a lot of fun.'

Rose Wild, *The Times*

'The Church of England has produced some real oddballs in its time, and this is an entertaining gallop through several centuries' worth of them... Butler-Gallie has done his homework, digging out some rare gems... This is the story not just of eccentrics, but also of a leisured age that is no more.'

Harry Mount, *Spectator*

A Field Guide to the English Clergy

A Compendium of *Diverse Eccentrics, Pirates, Prelates* and *Adventurers*; All Anglican, Some Even Practising

ONEWORLD

Fergus Butler-Gallie MA (Oxon), BA (Cantab), Clerk in Holy Orders

A Oneworld Book

First published by Oneworld Publications, 2018
This paperback edition published 2021, with a new Appendix by the author

ISBN 978-1-78607-574-1
eISBN 978-1-78607-442-3

Interior illustrations © Stephanie von Reiswitz

Typeset design by James Jones
Printed and bound in Great Britain by Clays Ltd, Elcograf S.p.A.

Oneworld Publications
10 Bloomsbury Street
London, WC1B 3SR
United Kingdom

Stay up to date with the latest books,
special offers, and exclusive content from
Oneworld with our newsletter

Sign up on our website
oneworld-publications.com

Dedication

The Author dedicates, with the utmost respect and humility,
this scraped together offering to both His Grace the ARCH-
BISHOP OF CANTERBURY and the DEAN OF CHRIST
CHURCH, OXON, so that, in mutual opprobrium at so
ghastly a volume, they might effect a THEOLOGICAL
RECONCILIATION befitting their respective
ranks and statures.

✠ ✠ ✠ Author's Note ✠ ✠ ✠

It will not escape the eagle-eyed reader that this is a compendium of eccentrics that features exclusively clergy of the male sex. Here, I'm afraid, your humble narrator can but plead cowardice. It is not that there is a shortage of eccentric, successful or nutty women, or, indeed, women renowned for their sense of adventure or love of good living currently in Holy Orders. However, the Church of England's regrettable tardiness in ordaining women to the Priesthood means that most of these potential subjects are still alive and, being women of great ingenuity as well as great godliness, many have access to excellent lawyers and some (particularly those in rural ministry) to unlicensed firearms. In light of this, a decision was made to restrict this collection to clergy who have shuffled off to a Better Place. It is to be hoped that the large numbers of women clergy who undoubtedly warrant a place in this collection will not feel too aggrieved by the author's decision to exclude the quick from his collection. Confident that God will continue to call as many manifestly strange women to the Priesthood as men, the author looks forward to a tome being produced in the not too distant future, replete with tales of these remarkable Priests; produced, however, by an individual braver (or with better legal representation) than he.

FBG
Cambridge, 2018

CONTENTS

BON VIVEURS

PRODIGAL SONS   99

ROGUES   137

ECCENTRICS

'The way of man is froward and strange'

Proverbs 21:8

The archetype of the dotty Anglican Vicar is one with enduring appeal. Whether the imagined parson of a half-remembered past or the character who gives a touch of anecdotal variety to the drudgery of parochial existence, a clergyman with unusual habits is a stock figure in the English cultural lexicon. The secret of the clerical eccentric's longevity in the popular imagination (long after it appears to have abandoned many of the other appendages of cultural Christianity) is that he is essentially a hybrid figure, standing at the crossroads of two rich seams of public strangeness. Put simply, to be a clergyman is eccentric enough, but to be English on top of that is almost overkill.

The parson is recognisably part of the broader tradition of English eccentricity. Quite what it is in the English character that has engendered such a predisposition is unclear – perhaps it is a legacy of those who seek to disrupt a culture historically bound by complex rules of etiquette and propriety, or maybe it's just a result of people trying to entertain themselves amid the perpetual drizzle. Either way, whether collecting curios, walking oddly or fostering inappropriate relationships with animals, the English have carved a niche as a nation with a streak of eccentricity running right through national life.

The Church of England is, of course, no exception. With its stated aim of ministering in every community and its presence at most of the stranger rituals of national life – from conducting coronations to judging competitions based around amusingly shaped vegetables – the Church, and its clergy, can justifiably claim to be the warp on which the mad tapestry of England has been woven.

Priests are part of a much older Christian vintage: that of the 'Holy Fool'. These were figures, particularly prevalent in the Eastern Orthodox tradition, who, through their odd behaviour, are said to make the rest of us consider where the real foolishness lies – namely in the ways of the world. The Holy Fool might seem strange in their behaviour to us, but, so the tradition says, it is in fact our ways that are strange. There is a concept, going back to the Gospels, of 'the Holy' being so inconceivable to limited human reasoning that it must appear to us as madness. It is a tradition that makes contemporary counterculture look positively mainstream. The great clerical eccentrics were undoubtedly considered to be insane or, at the very least, obsessive, and yet they often proved to be effective communicators of an 'other-worldly' holiness. It is partly the appeal of this, and partly the goodly heritage of old-fashioned Englishness that gives the eccentric Vicar his enduring appeal – he treads the thin line between prophet and clown.

The men whose lives are detailed in this section represent a mere tasting menu of eccentricity plucked from the rich à la carte selection of clerical strangeness down the ages. There was, alas, no room for figures such as the Cornish incumbent who was so prone to wandering off during services that he had to be chained to a communion rail by the ladies of the congregation. Nor was there space for the Lincolnshire clergyman who, fancying himself an amateur surgeon, got an elephant drunk on ale and tried to dissect it. However, the motley collection of mermaid-impersonating, steam-roller driving, bicycle-stealing clerics whose lives are detailed in the following pages are the cream of the crop, glorious in their eccentricities and their folly.

The eccentric Vicar is not, however, a figment of a half-imagined past. It might be the continued legacy of the Holy Fool or it might be something in the (Holy) water, but the Church of England is still replete with 'froward and strange' clergy to this day. While they are unlikely to follow in the footsteps of their forbears and urinate on you or force you to play leapfrog, they will undoubtedly be interesting, idiosyncratic figures – it rather comes with the territory. And so, dear reader, if you seek the great clerical eccentric, that fabled mid-point between Old English 'character' and Old Testament prophet, my advice is to look among the pews; they'll almost certainly be waiting for you there.

I

The Reverend Robert Hawker, Vicar of Morwenstow (1803–75)

The Mad Mermaid of Morwenstow

Cornwall, as a county of strange seascapes and moorland myths, has a remarkably high tolerance for odd behaviour.

However, even by the high bar of the West Country, the Reverend Robert Stephen Hawker was a profoundly weird individual. Hawker's behaviour, even as a youth, was the subject of considerable comment. Whether it was his running away from a series of schools or his marriage, while an undergraduate at Oxford aged just nineteen, to an old spinster, he showed early signs of not being exactly in line with the expectations of polite nineteenth-century society. However, it was his return to Cornwall as a clergyman that made him something of a local legend.

Firstly, as Curate at Bude, he decided that he had a joint calling; not only to be a Priest, but also a mermaid. In order to live out this vocation, he fashioned a wig out of seaweed and, naked apart from an oilskin wrapped around his legs, rowed out to a rock in Bude harbour one evening, sat on it and began to sing. This spectacle provoked great comment among superstitious locals and each evening a crowd gathered on the cliffs to see the 'mermaid' perform. Quite why this bizarre habit of Hawker's ended after a few months is debated; some say that, as the winter drew closer, even the blubbery form of Hawker was affected by the elements. Another story relates that a somewhat sceptical local farmer brought along his gun and threatened to pepper the aquatic damsel with shot if she stayed warbling any longer. Whatever the reason, one evening he substituted his haunting mermaid's lament for a rousing rendition of 'God Save the King', plopped into the water and swam back home.

After Bude, Hawker took on the vicarage of Morwenstow, a tiny parish at the most northerly tip of Cornwall. Here, devoid of supervision, he could indulge in his bizarre behaviour unabated. Although he no longer wore wigs made out of seaweed, his outfits were not exactly prim. Hawker would tramp around his parish wearing a long purple coat, a bright blue fisherman's jersey and red trousers stuffed into huge waterproof boots. In bad weather this extraordinary outfit was complemented by a bright yellow poncho made of horse hair that he dubiously claimed was the habit of an ancient Cornish saint. If any Vicar in history can be described as 'colourful', it is Hawker.

His time at Morwenstow was not without innovation; he famously invented the now ubiquitous harvest festival as a way of getting his parishioners (whom he viewed, perhaps not unfairly, as little more than baptised pagans) to come to church. Although clearly a great lover of landscapes, Hawker's relationship with the animate orders of creation was somewhat more complex. He kept a sizeable menagerie, including ten cats (who would follow him to church and routinely made up the majority of his congregation). However, he reacted with fury when he saw one catching a mouse on a Sunday and publicly excommunicated it in front of his other animals. Sabbath day violations aside, Hawker was a great lover of animals, being regularly observed talking to the birds in the churchyard and making friends with a 'highly intelligent' pig called Gyp. Another 'pet' was a stag called Robin, which Hawker insisted was tame, although its habit of attacking and pinning down visitors to the vicarage would probably suggest otherwise.

Hawker was not without a sense of clerical duty. He made it his particular mission to collect the bodies of sailors who regularly drowned in shipwrecks off the treacherous north Cornish coast. He was also assiduous in improving the parish, rebuilding the dilapidated vicarage out of his own pocket, although he did insist on designing the building himself, resulting in an odd-looking structure where the chimney pots were modelled on his favourite towers, one of which used the same design as his mother's gravestone. In his later years he tried to raise funds to rebuild the church as well, but his track record of strange behaviour and his growing opium addiction made him a less than attractive investment prospect. During this time he also wrote a bizarre poem about an imprisoned Bishop called 'The Song of the Western Men' (now more widely known as 'Trelawny', the unofficial Cornish anthem). In 1875, he died, short on hard cash, but still full of airy ideas.

If you visit Morwenstow today you will see signposts pointing to the intriguingly named 'Hawker's Hut'. Built by the parson out of driftwood from shipwrecks, he would sit for hours in a haze of opiates, happily chattering away to the birds and writing nonsensical poetry. It has the unusual distinction of being the smallest property in the possession of the National Trust, a testament to the abiding appeal of the strange life of Robert Hawker as well as a suitably unique accolade, of which the great merman might be proud.

II

The Reverend George Harvest,
Rector of Thames Ditton (1728–89)

'The Most Forgetful Man in England'

George Harvest was known by contemporaries as 'the most forgetful man in England'. This was putting it kindly; Harvest was, in fact, nothing short of a human disaster zone, whose absent-mindedness reached such prolific levels that whole chapters of his ministry read like the script for a farce. Harvest was from a wealthy background and, having obtained the usual degree at Oxford, prepared to take Holy Orders. His sizeable income and good prospects meant that he was lined up to marry the daughter of the Bishop of London while still a humble Curate. Indeed, she went so far as to accept a proposal and plans were made for an impressive society wedding, to be officiated by the bride's father – Harvest's boss. The day arrived and, in a flurry of Austen-esque excitement, the bridal party began preparations. In stark contrast, the groom had woken up and, struck by a sudden desire to catch gudgeons (a type of small river fish), had packed up his rod and lures and set off to find a suitable spot. It is not known exactly when Harvest realised his mistake, suffice to say by the time he hurried to the church, his marriage, and any prospect of future promotion, were in tatters.

After such a catastrophic foray into the world of romance, you might imagine that the Rector of Thames Ditton (a post he had finally procured through the charity of a powerful friend) had learned his lesson. You would be wrong. Harvest (somehow) managed to set a date for another marriage ceremony with a second unfortunate fiancée. However, on the day in question, when the carriage called to pick him up, he was nowhere to be found. Several hours later, as Harvest was midway through supper with some people he'd met on a morning stroll to Richmond, he realised that he was meant to be doing something rather more important that day. He rushed back, only to find another sobbing bride and another furious father. Apparently informing the offended party that it had been 'one of the pleasantest walks of my life' did nothing to effect a reconciliation and Harvest remained a bachelor.

In fairness to Harvest, his betrothed had known what she was letting herself in for. Earlier on in their relationship,

Harvest had forgotten that he was supposed to be meeting her one morning and had slept in. Subsequently, he decided, showcasing the appalling decision-making that was to become his trademark, that it would be easier to shave himself en route rather than waste time at the rectory. All went well for Harvest until he reached the end of the lane, where his fiancée's house was located. Here he stopped and, resting his shaving kit on his saddle, proceeded with his ablutions. Remarkably, the actual shaving went to plan; however, when Harvest tried to pack his things away, his horse took fright and ran down the lane, with a topless, soapy Harvest on top of her, scattering toiletries as they went. In the end the mare came to a stop just outside the young lady's house, where she and her family were still waiting outside to meet the great catch.

Horses were particularly forgettable for Harvest, and not a single person in three counties was prepared to lend him one for even a couple of hours, after a series of incidents where the clergyman would return to the stables dragging a rein and bridle along the floor, with no explanation as to how he had managed to misplace the animal he had been riding. Indeed, almost anything was at risk in Harvest's possession. A friend recounted a visit to London where Harvest found an interesting pebble near the Thames. He picked it up and put it in his pocket in order to show it to a mutual acquaintance later on. Some minutes later, Harvest's friend asked the time. Harvest took out his expensive pocket watch and duly obliged. The friend then watched in silent horror as the clergyman absentmindedly skimmed the timepiece across the surface of the Thames. It was only some hours later, when he tried to check the time on his shiny pebble, that Harvest realised what had happened.

Harvest's erratic behaviour affected not only his personal life but his professional one, too. On several occasions, after hearing a great noise in his church while lumbering round the graveyard, he ran home to fetch a gun and surprise the intruders. Harvest would burst in with his firearm, only to find a stunned congregation sitting waiting to begin the Sunday service (which the Rector had, naturally, forgotten). The congregation were not entirely passive victims of their Priest's eccentricities, it being considered great sport among them to secrete various unrelated pieces of paper into the pages of Harvest's sermon and watch him read them out. On one occasion the entire congregation slowly slipped out of the back of the church during the course of a particularly long homily, with Harvest only noticing when the Churchwarden told him he was going to lock up; on another he read out a rude poem in lieu of the banns of marriage and then became enormously confused when the congregation burst out laughing.

Perhaps his finest pastoral moment came when he was asked to explain the constellations of the night sky to Lady Onslow (the wife of the friend who had got him his job). Midway through Harvest's explanation, the noble lady suddenly felt a warm and damp sensation at her feet; Harvest, pressed by a call of nature, had taken advantage of the cover afforded by the darkness of the night and begun to relieve himself while continuing his astronomical lecture. Unfortunately for Lady Onslow, Harvest had mixed up his left and right and, while he thought he was surreptitiously urinating away from her (itself a less than ideal situation) he was, in fact, detailing the wonders of the Plough while passing water down her leg. After his death in Thames Ditton in 1789, a contemporary author was surely correct when he described Harvest as a divine whose character was 'of such a singular composition that we shall scarcely find its equal'. Whether it was twice missing his marriage, pointing a pistol at his parishioners or pissing on a peeress, Harvest was unlike any other cleric the Church of England has ever seen.

III

The Reverend Sandys Wason,
Perpetual Curate of Cury and Gunwalloe (1867–1950)

Sci-fi, Sermons and a Donkey Called Sheila

One of the many concepts that the modern church has borrowed from secular office jargon is 'collaborative leadership'. These days it is the norm for clergymen to be expected to demonstrate that they are a 'team player'. Leighton Sandys Wason was not, however, a 'team player'. Whether it was publicly disrespecting his Bishop or ignoring the dirty protests of his congregants, Wason gave the studied impression of living in another world. In many ways, he did, as he was a prolific author of nonsense verse and an early pioneer in the genre of science fiction. Yet even his penchant for producing fantastical stories cannot explain his flagrant disregard for the opinions of every soul he met.

Wason was born to a relatively prosperous family in Marylebone in 1867 and, after school, went up to Christ Church, Oxford, to study. *Fin de siècle* Oxford was awash with the self-consciously extreme Anglo-Catholics ('sodomites with unpleasant funny accents' as Evelyn Waugh so memorably termed them in *Brideshead Revisited*). Wason embraced both eccentricity and Anglo-Catholicism, attending Mass daily and taking to wearing a monocle, despite having perfectly good eyesight. Ordination was the next step and, from 1894 to 1897, Wason was Curate of the Suffolk village of Elmswell. Here he prayed using rosary beads, installed statues of the Virgin Mary and lobbied to have every service said in Latin; all seemingly harmless to modern sensibilities, but very much illegal under the law of a Church still partially scarred by the legacy of the Reformation. His very public love of Catholic devotions made it impossible for the Bishop to advance him beyond the position of Deacon and ordain him Priest, as he was, daily, contravening the law of the Church of England. Unperturbed, Wason moved to Plaistow in the East End of London where a more sympathetic (or less assiduous) Bishop agreed to ordain him.

This Bishop soon realised his mistake and made clear to Wason that there was no chance of him ever securing a parish of his own unless he changed his extreme practices. Wason, once again, stuck two fingers up at his superiors and went to the one diocese in England where communications were so poor and discipline so lax that he might have been able to get away with doing what he wanted: Truro. The inhabitants of the tiny villages of Cury and Gunwalloe on the Lizard peninsula can hardly have known what had hit them. After being provisionally made Priest in charge of the two hamlets, Wason immediately set to work turning them into centres of Catholic worship that rivalled even Rome. He didn't give a fig for cost, using money from his mother's will to install (without permission) a solid, marble altar in place of the wooden communion table which, when diocesan officials arrived to remove it, proved so sizeable as to be totally intractable and so remains there to this day. Wason also didn't care what his parishioners thought. The English are not usually keen on 'long religion' and so Wason's Sunday services, which consisted of several Masses (each taking two hours at a bare minimum and often in Latin), followed by benediction of the blessed sacrament and a public recital of the rosary, were not exactly popular.

Wason would probably have been disciplined earlier had the First World War not intervened (he spent the conflict trying to stir up anti-Protestant feeling in the villages on the sole basis that the Reformation had begun in Germany). However, by 1919, even the inhabitants of this quiet corner of Cornwall had had enough. A group began to disrupt Wason's services, preaching loudly outside and rattling the door of the church (which Wason usually kept locked) to disturb the rites inside. On one occasion, Wason was striding out of the church when a man asked him how he could keep his own parishioners locked out (he had a point: this, like much of Wason's practice, was illegal). Wason simply strode past, his cassock billowing, pushing the heckler into a ditch as he went. Later on, his parishioners even went so far as to dig up the body of a recently deceased donkey called Sheila and dump her on Wason's front doorstep like Cornish Mafiosi. The following morning Wason opened the door of the vicarage, took one look at Sheila's putrefying remains, drew up his cassock, stepped over the unfortunate creature and carried on his way to church as usual.

Eventually, the parish had had enough and appealed to the Bishop. The Bishop, underestimating Wason's sheer determination, reasoned that a visit by his superior might convince Cury and Gunwalloe's Priest of the gravity of the situation. Accordingly, the Bishop arranged to have a notice put on the church door at Cury announcing that he would celebrate a church service there on the morning of Sunday 1 June 1919. When the Bishop arrived the following morning, he found that Wason had scribbled out his advertised service times and instead written 'MASS & BENEDICTION – 11AM' over the top of them. Sensing that things weren't going to be as easy as he'd hoped, the Bishop gingerly opened the door of the church and entered, followed by a crowd of bemused parishioners. Wason had just finished the Mass and was now in the midst of a sermon. The sermon, which Wason would routinely interrupt to shout at people he thought were moving too much or making unnecessary noise, lasted until nearly half past two, the Bishop having given up by five past. At three o'clock, he began the two-hour-long evensong and benediction, with the final combined service time standing at six hours.

The Bishop, unsurprisingly, fired Wason but he refused to leave, steadfastly ignoring the dead animals that found their way to his doorstep. However, on 2 October 1919, Wason went to the entrance of the vicarage and answered what he thought was a sick call. Instead, when he opened the door he found a large group of burly Cornishmen who promptly packed him into a waiting car and dumped him in a neighbouring village.

Wason had no hope of holding an ecclesiastical office again and so turned to writing. His poetry was deliberately nonsensical. One piece, which, for some reason, he gave the German title *Kabale und Liebe*, contains such bizarre images as 'the omelette of the past' and compares 'nicotine extravaganzas' to 'a cheese at evening'. More successful than his surreal poems was his foray into science fiction, with his 1927 work *Palafox*, which imagined a device that could read other people's thoughts, ensuring that he didn't die totally bankrupt. It is ironic that a novel with such a theme could have redeemed the fortunes of a man who spent his clerical career demonstrating that he had no ability to relate to the thoughts of other people whatsoever.

IV

The Reverend Thomas Massey,
Rector of Farringdon (c.1829–1919)

Phobias, Photography and the Largest Folly in Britain

Many clergy complain that a huge amount of their time is taken up not with ministering to their flock, but with the prosaic issue of caring for unwieldy and strangely designed buildings. Of no one was this more true than the Reverend Thomas Hackett Massey. Massey, however, didn't spend his marathon sixty-two-year stint as Vicar of Farringdon in Hampshire on conventional building projects but instead, ignoring most of his parish responsibilities, devoted his time to building an enormous house, the architectural plans for which changed on a daily basis. The resulting higgledy-piggledy pile of bricks remains to this day as a testament to the bizarre plans of a clergyman who, even by the remarkable standards of the Victorians, was considered distinctly strange.

Massey began his lengthy term in charge of the spiritual and moral welfare of Farringdon in 1857. Even before construction started on the folly his behaviour was far from typical. Massey developed an irrational fear of the new technology of photography, even going so far as to conduct his church services while sitting behind a screen lest an enterprising parishioner decide to play paparazzo. He developed a habit of throwing coins at the children of the parish who responded by rushing the Rector and pushing him into nearby ditches on more than one occasion. Then, after a decade in post, it became clear that the parish church of All Saints needed some work doing on its fabric. Massey began to oversee the necessary repairs only to turn up one morning in 1870 and fire all but three of the workforce. Massey took his nominated carpenter, bricklayer and general dogsbody to a field across the road and set them to work on an entirely new project – the gargantuan edifice that would become known as 'Massey's Folly'.

Massey's insistence on building most of the folly with his own hands, allowing for occasional help from his three labourers, meant that progress was painstakingly slow. The speed was not helped by Massey's insistence on regularly changing his plans; he would turn up and begin demolishing completed parts of the building for no apparent reason. By the late 1870s, Massey was totally absorbed in his unusual construction project and spent next to no time on his parish responsibilities, a situation that would continue until his death in 1919. Given the inordinate complexity of the project, one could be forgiven for thinking that Massey had some clear idea in his mind with regard to the purpose of the building. However, such is the intricacy of the design and the preponderance of staircases and corridors that lead nowhere, that no permanent use has ever been found for it. Some maintain that the entire project was nothing more than an attempt by Massey to impress a local widow recently returned from a life among the palaces of the Raj, while others claim he was convinced that Farringdon was destined to become a major conurbation in the twentieth century and so wanted to build an impressive town hall before the developers arrived.

Massey himself was less than helpful about his intentions

for the building. Perhaps understandably, the strangeness of such a major building project in such a small village excited the attentions of the press. Massey agreed to speak to a journalist from the newspaper based in nearby Alton (on the proviso, of course, that no photographs were to be taken). When asked about the purpose of the palatial edifice Massey replied cryptically, 'It is going to be a tea room, with a red globe on the tower that will turn green when the tea is brewed.' No such globe was ever installed, suggesting that Massey was making a joke at the expense of a credulous journalist.

When Massey died in 1919, with the building still technically under construction, any chance of discerning its actual purpose was lost forever. What is not in doubt is its scale – it remains the largest folly in Britain. Since the Rector's death, it has served as a working men's club, a nursery school and a cabaret venue (though not simultaneously). In 2016, developers began converting the folly into a complex of flats, giving the structure its first clearly designated purpose in well over a hundred years. Whether the developers will be installing the magic red/green tea globe, as stipulated by its original architect, remains to be seen.

V

The Right Reverend Lord William Cecil, Bishop of Exeter (1863–1936)

'A shaggy head and woolly mind'

Sent to Eton at an early age, William there acquired the name 'Fish' due to his persistent gormlessness. With the admirable pastoral intuition for which the English aristocracy is renowned, when his family learned of the nickname used to torment William at school, they promptly adopted it as well. After receiving one of the worst marks ever recorded by a student in his law degree at Oxford, William somehow fell into Holy Orders – possibly helped along by his father, Prime Minister Lord Salisbury – and ended up as the Vicar of Hatfield, near the ancestral home of the Marquesses of Salisbury, where his father could keep an eye on him.

And there William would have remained had a number of strange coincidences not intervened. In 1916, the then Bishop of Exeter took advantage of new legislation and retired, drawing an enormous pension worth a third of the diocese's income until his eventual death in 1931. On top of this local financial crisis, Herbert Asquith was now pretty busy with the small matter of the First World War, and so episcopal appointments were not top of his list. Civil servants dug out the name of one of the only clergymen capable of supporting himself as a Bishop by private means and so, in 1916, 'Fish' was made Bishop of Exeter.

Cecil's eccentricity was noted almost immediately. He made an early impact when he absentmindedly threw a large quantity of copper sulphate on the fire in his study while meeting senior diocesan clergy, remarking as his colleagues cowered behind the furniture, staring at the green flames, that he 'liked the colour'. Visits to the Palace became something of a social minefield. The Dean's wife, invited to take tea with the Bishop, related her shock when Cecil removed the plate of crumpets provided and proceeded to feed them to two rats that appeared, on cue, out of holes in the floor. His presence at services was at least as bizarre – prior to one Holy Communion he placed a handkerchief in his mouth for safe-keeping as his hands were full, only to emerge from the vestry and begin the service with the dirty piece of fabric still hanging from his mouth.

Cecil was more dangerous when allowed out of the immediate confines of the cathedral close. Once, when he had somehow managed to become separated from a procession he was meant to be leading in a rural parish, he accosted a terrified villager, bellowing, 'Which way did the hounds go!?' His normal course of action when he found himself somewhere and had forgotten why was to ring his wife – many a Devon postmistress had stories of the bearded Bishop barging in, demanding use of a telephone in order to work out where he was. This habit of well-intended house-breaking, along with his penchant for 'borrowing' bicycles, earned him a new nickname: 'Burglar Bill'.

His fixation with bicycles became quite a serious problem. After being driven to one diocesan appointment in a car he mysteriously returned on a woman's bike. Such was his horror at this accidental theft that he immediately rang the police, found out the owner and pedalled into Exeter to return it. He placed the bike against a wall, apologised to its owner and then promptly rode off on it again back to the Palace. Eventually his wife and Chaplains conspired to paint his own bicycle bright red in order to distinguish it from other Exonian velocipedes. (The colour eventually had to be changed to a canary-yellow after the Bishop returned with a series of postmen's bicycles, complete with undelivered post.)

Along with 'Burglar Bill' and 'Fish', Cecil acquired the nickname 'Love in a Mist', as a result of his fuzzy thinking and general ineptitude. Somewhat problematically, he could also be something of an autocrat, being by equal measures angry and confused when he didn't get his own way. After one particularly stormy encounter with the chapter of the cathedral he tried to abolish the position of Dean altogether, only to calm down and repent some days later. He was also heard asking whether something could be done about 'that awkward book' after a theological discussion didn't go his way. He was referring, of course, to the Bible.

Despite his simian appearance and bizarre behaviour, Cecil was well loved by the people of Devon (except, perhaps, those who were cyclists). When he died in 1936 they clubbed together to commission a memorial in the cathedral he had not long before threatened to shut down. A plaque near the monument expresses the wish that it might 'keep alive forever the memory of William Cecil'. The people of Devon can, I think, rest easy: whether it is for bike-burgling, house-breaking or his forays into domestic chemistry, there is little chance of such a figure being forgotten.

VI

The Reverend Edwin 'Teddy' Boston, Rector of Cadeby cum Sutton Cheney (1924–86)

Steamrollers and Strong Language – the Man Who Inspired 'The Fat Controller'

Few scenes are considered more typical of a certain lost era of England than of a steam train chugging past a country church; it is the sort of faintly twee image that sends jigsaw makers and tea cosy producers into fits of rapture. However, for the Reverend Edwin Boston the marriage of church and steam was no *People's Friend* fantasy but, rather, the focus of his ministry for nearly forty years. The expression 'larger than life' might have been designed for the corpulent clergyman. Whether it was turning up impromptu at strangers' houses to view their model trains, his rigorous use of 'Anglo-Saxon' language while driving, or his insistence on running his daily errands using a steamroller as his primary mode of transport, the joyful chaos wrought by Teddy Boston resulted in a life peppered with steam-related incidents that were about as far removed from the chocolate-box stereotype as could be.

Edwin Boston was born in 1924 and, after an unexceptional period at Cambridge, was ordained in 1949. Boston was what we might call 'a big kid' (both in terms of maturity and frame) and was fond of quoting Matthew 18:3 – 'unless you become as little children, ye shall not enter the kingdom of heaven' – as an excuse when anyone (often his wife) became exasperated by his latest hare-brained scheme. But it wasn't until he took up the position of Rector to the two tiny Leicestershire villages of Cadeby and Sutton Cheney that Teddy really had a chance to indulge his lifelong obsession with steam trains. In 1962 he made the impulsive purchase of a steam engine that was set to be scrapped, which he named 'Pixie'. Fortunately, the rectory came with a sizeable garden and it wasn't long before Boston had constructed his own railway track and was merrily steaming round his garden on Pixie, to the delight of many of his parishioners.

However, Pixie was only the beginning. Not long after constructing the railway track in his garden, Teddy managed to buy a decrepit steam engine in Shropshire which he named 'the Terror'. This was followed by a massive steam-roller, christened 'Thistledown'. Eventually, Boston restored both locomotives and the steamroller, and the latter became his steed. One visitor to Cadeby rectory described how, with Teddy involved, even a simple trip to the shops became a major logistical operation. Teddy would cruise along the narrow lanes of Leicestershire, oblivious to the traffic which, even in those relatively car-free days, must have been backing up behind him, before making his way into Market Bosworth and plonking the steamroller in the middle of the square while he went about his errands.

It wasn't only machines of great size that captured Teddy's imagination – he was just as obsessed with miniature railways, and he would scour the country trying to find the best examples. The Reverend W. Awdry (another clerical steam enthusiast who wrote the *Thomas the Tank Engine* books), described how he first met Teddy when he appeared unannounced at his rectory demanding to see the model railway that Awdry had constructed in his study. Despite his impromptu arrival, Teddy and Awdry became great friends, with the chubby rector of Cadeby serving as the inspiration for 'The Fat Controller' and 'The Fat Clergyman' in Awdry's famous Thomas stories. When he wasn't barging into strangers' houses to look at their model railways, he was building a vast one of his own, painstakingly recreating the stretch of the Great Western Railway between Newton Abbot and Totnes in Devon as it stood in 1935 (although he never divulged why he was quite so specific in the design) in an enormous shed in his garden.

While his interests were staggeringly niche, Teddy undeniably had the common touch. From his astonishing range of swear words, often deployed just as he was about to derail into a hedge, to his sheer joy whenever someone asked if they could see his back garden, his larger than life spirit made him enormously popular in the parish. In the end his urge to share his trains with the world was so great that he opened up the rectory as a sort of museum. It was described by one visitor as 'a place where anything could happen, and usually did'. Teddy ran the whole operation, waddling to and fro in his oil-soaked overalls and clerical collar. Minor accidents were common, such as when Teddy managed to crash Pixie in such a way that all her wheels fell off at once. When Teddy finally died in 1986 he was mourned not only by his parishioners, but by many across the country to whom he had, in his own erratic way, shown kindness. If you go into Cadeby church today, you will find a rather strange stained-glass window. It depicts the outline of a distinctly portly figure driving a steam train, on which one can just about make out a plaque that reads 'Pixie'.

VII

The Reverend Frederick Densham, Vicar of Warleggan (1870–1953)

Bananas and Barbed Wire on Bodmin Moor

Contrary to what some theologians would like to believe, the Church has much in common with secular organisations. Perhaps the most unfortunate of these commonalities, at least for an institution that seeks to focus on the Divine, is that it is made up of humans. As such, it is as susceptible to human error and to that most human of phenomena, breakdowns in relationships. Few institutions, however, can claim a breakdown in relations as catastrophic as that between the Reverend Frederick Densham and his congregation.

Densham was the son of a Methodist minister but, for reasons lost in the mists of time, became an Anglican and eventually took Holy Orders after studying in London and Oxford. After a long career spent as a missionary, in South Africa and India but also in Whitechapel, in the East End of London, where he helped run a home for the chronically inebriated, Densham made the curious decision to take up the living of Warleggan, a tiny, windswept hamlet of 168 souls on the edge of Bodmin Moor, Cornwall. Warleggan itself is an idiosyncratic enough place (it holds the peculiar distinction of being twinned with the fictional location of C. S. Lewis's Narnia). However, even the unusual denizens of this isolated part of Cornwall were unprepared for the strange beast who entered their midst in 1931.

Densham began a series of 'improvements' almost as soon as he arrived at Warleggan. His first project was to paint the ancient interior of St Bartholomew's church, which had been largely untouched since the Reformation, in garish primary colours (an act which he was later forced painstakingly to reverse by order of the Bishop). Other projects included the total abolition of Sunday School and a sermon series on the great benefits of vegetarianism (Densham practised what he preached, eating just one meal a day, which consisted of porridge with a side dish of boiled stinging nettles). The sermons proved about as popular as one might expect among a congregation who were just managing to eke out a living through farming livestock. Relations were further strained as Densham revealed his plans for removing the organ based on his belief that music was a 'gabbled profanity' and an 'amusement from Hell'.

Organ music was only one of a long list of things (which included the cinema, reading and the card game whist) that Densham thought were inventions of Satan. Fortunately for music lovers in Warleggan, Densham was dissuaded from his plan to dismantle and burn the organ, but only when his Churchwarden informed him that, if he touched it, he would punch the Vicar in the face.

It took only two years for the villagers to become so frustrated that they contacted the Bishop and requested Densham's removal. To be fair to the churchgoing folk of Warleggan, alongside his eccentricities and awkwardness Densham made it quite clear that his personal ecclesiastical preferences lay elsewhere. He would routinely hold services at deliberately difficult times in order to be able to attend the village's Methodist chapel as an ordinary member of the congregation. Densham's 'Low Church' Methodist sympathies were out of step with the 'High Church' tradition of the village and, eventually, after an ignominious argument over a whist drive and the Bishop's refusal to entertain their complaints, the good people of Warleggan voted with their feet and simply ceased to attend the few, inconvenient services that Densham bothered to conduct. Densham paid no attention to this exodus, instead replacing his absent parishioners with cards on which he had written the names of former vicars – a collection he liked to call his 'congregation of ghosts'. Each Sunday, Densham would arrange these pieces of card in his brightly coloured pews and conduct worship as if they really were his congregation. After the service he would dutifully fill in the parish attendance register, often adding little comments as he did so; one such annotation reads, 'Sunday – no wind, no rain, no fog, no congregation'. The lack of congregation can hardly have been a surprise to him, given that he had devoted large amounts of his time to installing increasingly elaborate locking mechanisms on the church doors.

It wasn't only the church that Densham made inaccessible to his parishioners. He installed an eight-foot barbed wire fence around the perimeter of the vicarage, inside of which he kept nearly a dozen Alsatians. While Densham did install a small gong by the gate in the fence, if parishioners rang it, they invariably succeeded only in provoking the wrath of the dogs inside. Those who did manage to gain entry had to navigate their way around the equally strange alterations that Densham had made to the interior of the building. One part of the house was converted into an elaborate sanctuary, while a whole room in another section was given over to Densham's collection of nettle-based food and drink products.

During the Second World War, Densham became convinced the Third Reich would target his tiny Cornish hamlet with all the resources at its disposal. In response to this perceived threat, Densham converted a sizeable chunk of the vicarage into a field hospital, filling rooms with bandages, medical supplies and industrial quantities of Vaseline. For those who did make their way to the Vicar's cramped living quarters, the reward was not exactly enticing, with Densham's version of dinner party cuisine being a cup of nettle tea and a plate of mouldy bananas.

The stalemate between Densham and his parishioners continued until the Vicar's death in 1953. As long as he turned up and gave his services, it was very difficult for the Bishop to remove him, even if nobody else was there. The long-running dispute eventually came to the attention of the press. Densham was even interviewed by an American newspaper in the run-up to his final Christmas in 1952. He told the journalist that he had no intention of giving up as 'they all come back to me in the end; I conduct all the funerals'.

A few months later, it was Densham himself who was dead. There were very few mourners at his funeral, but, after his passing, tales of his kindness to the sick and unfortunate of the village began to emerge. The village did, however, frustrate their Vicar one final time. As a clear sign of his unwillingness to budge, Densham had selected a spot for his ashes back in the early 1930s. Over the years he constructed a bizarre, barbed wire-clad garden of remembrance in the grounds of the vicarage, only for the church council to refuse his request to have his ashes buried there. The Vicar, however, is not forgotten in Warleggan; there are villagers who swear that Densham's spirit still wanders between the old vicarage and the church. We might say that he has gone to join the 'congregation of ghosts'.

VIII

The Reverend Ian Graham-Orlebar, Rector of Barton-le-Clay (1926–2016)

Bedfordshire's Equestrian Throwback

We live in an age where retro is the new modern. Be it sticking an inflated price tag on a charity shop piece and calling it vintage, or the return of those political movements that made the twentieth century such an unbounded delight – at present, the past is the future. The fantastically named Ian Henry Gaunt Graham-Orlebar discerned that it was his particular ministry to live a life that was self-consciously retro. As Vicar of Barton-le-Clay in rural Bedfordshire, he enthusiastically embraced the role of the throwback and, well into the twenty-first century, adopted a lifestyle and persona that a country parson in the age of Jane Austen would be proud of.

Born into comfortable circumstances in 1926, Graham-Orlebar (known as 'Nin' to his family and friends) was initially destined for a legal career. Having studied law at New College, Oxford, he spent a decade working, with considerable financial success, as a solicitor in London. However, a calling to the Priesthood bubbled to the surface and Nin abandoned the legal profession in 1962 in order to be ordained. He served as a Curate in the glamorous setting of Hemel Hempstead, Hertfordshire, where, happy and un-ambitious, he remained for eight years. However, in 1970 he was contacted by the Bishop of St Albans (future Archbishop of Canterbury, Robert Runcie) with a strange proposition.

The living of Barton-le-Clay, for which Runcie was responsible, had recently become vacant. The job was something of a poisoned chalice as the villagers had made clear that they wanted a Rector who could maintain the house that came with the job. This might seem reasonable enough; however, the rectory at Barton was a great, rambling mansion, with acres of grounds that had previously kept a number of full-time gardeners employed, entire wings of huge reception rooms and a moat. The average cleric had neither the willpower nor the resources to keep such a levi-athan in order; Ian Graham-Orlebar, however, was not the average cleric. He accepted Runcie's offer and immediately set to work turning the rectory into a residence fit for a gentleman parson of yore. Conscripting the younger mem-bers of the church choir as manual labour, Nin proceeded to clear the moat, restock the lake with fish and, in an act of ecumenical mischief, even constructed an elaborate bridge using stonework that he'd pinched from the ruins of a near-by Methodist chapel.

With the restoration of the rectory complete, Graham-Orlebar settled into the role of a country parson. A keen equestrian since his boyhood, Barton-le-Clay's new Priest decided that, in homage to the dignified clergy of old, he would conduct all visits on horseback. Stating his disdain for what he called 'modern motorised parsons' (although, in his later years, he made some concessions in this regard and was often observed travelling about on his ride-on lawnmower), Nin would merrily trot around his parish calling out to anyone he met, churchgoer or not. His sense of mischief was evident in his nomenclature for these beasts of burden: his first horse was called 'Ministry' so that, when an Archdeacon or other senior figure telephoned the rectory to check up on him, they could be truthfully informed by his maid that he was 'exercising his Ministry'. After Ministry was dispatched to the big glue factory in the sky, Graham-Orlebar set about finding a suitable name for her replacement. Naturally he turned to that infallible oracle of Middle England for an answer – the letters page of the *Daily Telegraph*. Suggestions poured in and, when clergy callers pestered the rectory, from then on they would be told that the rector was out 'on Sabbatical'.

His love of pranks was infamous. When Britain joined what was then known as the European Economic Community in 1973, he felt that, in the style of the infallible rectors of old, it was his duty to arrange an information evening to educate his parish about this momentous event. His love of mischief, however, got the better of him and so he gravely informed his parishioners that new regulations meant that the day would now have ten rather than twenty-four hours (producing a specially adapted clock to demonstrate) and that the highway code had been changed, rendering driving on the right compulsory and round-abouts obsolete, resulting in a short and very localised spell of chaos on the roads of south Bedfordshire. In another act of mischief, he made headlines in the local press when he informed a provincial newspaper that a rare breed of duck 'with powerful bills' was eating its way through the stones of the rectory rockery.

Alongside his affectations, Graham-Orlebar was an incredibly effective Priest. His palatial home was open to all the parish, with long corridors being used for youth club games and the gardens for parish picnics; his horses were not only to perpetuate the Austen-era caricature but also enabled him to run the local Riding for the Disabled group. After a happy and long ministry, Graham-Orlebar retired to Devon. He found it impossible, however, to stay still for too long and deliberately bought a house with a sizeable garden, which was almost immediately opened to the public. It is hardly surprising that he was organising an enormous ninetieth birthday for himself when he died in 2016. A throwback and deliberate caricature he may have been, but there can be no doubt that he was successful in 'exercising his Ministry'.

IX

The Reverend Morgan Jones,
Curate of Blewbury (1747–1827)

The Miser of Blewbury

The saying 'as poor as a church mouse' gives an accurate description of the financial status of most clergy today.

Realistically, despite historic and contemporary assertions about the great wealth of the Church, ordinary parish clergy have never been paid well. Nobody in their right mind would enter Holy Orders with the intention of getting rich. And so we have to wonder about the Reverend Morgan Jones. After a gruelling forty-three years as perpetual Curate of Blewbury, a tiny village on the border between Oxfordshire and Berkshire, Jones, by adopting a lifestyle of extreme parsimony, contrived to save a massive £18,000, worth a small fortune in today's money.

Jones was, it will come as no surprise to learn, a Welshman, who, having been ordained in his native country, came to Blewbury in 1781 via a spell as Curate in Ashton Keynes in Wiltshire. Signs of Jones's penny pinching were evident even at this early juncture as he arrived in the parish looking, as one contemporary put it, 'much the worse for wear'. Jones's coat was said to be in a particularly objectionable state but, if his new parishioners thought they might cajole their new clergyman into buying a new one, they were much mistaken. Jones ended up wearing that coat for the following forty-three years, turning it inside out, sewing patchwork onto it, doing anything, in fact, to avoid buying a new one. Jones's efforts in this were successful – the threadbare jacket (as it became after he ripped off the coat-tails in order to repair the sleeves) survived Jones himself and was kept well into the Victorian period as a local curiosity.

Jones was adamant that his tiny stipend of less than £100 a year could be stretched to enable him to accrue a small fortune. Alongside his famous coat, the miserly clergyman also refused to buy a new hat, even when the brim of his old one disintegrated completely one day when he raised it to a passing lady. The ever-resourceful Jones spent the next couple of days scouring the fields near Blewbury until he happened upon a scarecrow equipped with a hat in a considerably better condition than his own. Overjoyed at having found a way out of paying for a new piece of head-gear, the Curate borrowed the scarecrow's hat, removed its brim and sewed it onto his own. The fact that this newly pilfered piece of millinery was black while the old hat was a sort of sludgy brown didn't bother Jones in the slightest. This mismatch of fabrics and colours naturally earned the cleric comparisons with the biblical Joseph (of multicoloured coat fame). Although they were somewhat battered, at least Jones wore his hat and coat. The same cannot always be said for a shirt as, unwilling to buy more than one, Jones would routinely wander round the parish topless when this solitary garment happened to be in the wash.

It wasn't only in his personal appearance that Jones cut corners to save money. In managing his domestic affairs he was equally parsimonious, running his household according to the principle that there are only two 'essentials' in life: bread and bacon. He did also allow himself one 'luxury', a small amount of tea, which he would drink as a treat on Sunday mornings. He would purchase his bacon on a Saturday, cook it all on Sunday and then carefully apportion it during the rest of the week. It would have been nigh-on impossible for anyone, even an individual as austere as Jones, to survive exclusively on such a diet and so, taking full advantage of his responsibility for the cure of souls in Blewbury, Jones often timed a 'pastoral visit' to coincide with his parishioners' supper. Jones was known for his ability to put away enormous amounts of food and of ale, despite the fact that he was not known to have spent a single penny on beer during his whole ministry in Blewbury. Fond though he was of ale and fine dining at other people's expense, he just couldn't bring himself to indulge his taste for them when it entailed spending even a penny of his own. Given his lack of practical clothing, it can be of no surprise that Jones was often in need of a fire in order to warm himself. Once again, though, the thought of spending money on what he termed 'a luxury' (in this case wood or coal) was more than he could bear. Instead, he was often observed picking up sticks that fell from the trees in the churchyard, sneaking into his parishioners' gardens to snap off low-lying branches and even rummaging through rubbish heaps in order to find appropriate (free) fuel for his fire.

Though he was a miser of the highest order, Jones was generally considered a good Priest. His sermons were thought particularly fine, even though they were invariably written on whichever scraps of paper he had managed to pick up from around the village. Someone even went as far as to recommend that Jones might publish some of them, a suggestion he considered, only to reject it after he lost a full night's sleep worrying over the potential postage costs that such a project would incur.

Eventually, in 1824, Jones retired and, having been unable to find anyone in his parish who would allow him to live with them for free, he was forced to return to Wales to move in with some distant relatives. These unfortunates were said to be more than a little put out by the bedraggled cleric's arrival and somewhat dubious of his claims that they would be rewarded in his will. Imagine their surprise, therefore, when, on Jones's death three years later, they received a cheque for nearly £18,000, about £1.5 million today. The story of the millionaire parson who lived like a beggar soon attracted widespread attention, with a young Charles Dickens being so captivated by the tale that he based the character of Blewbury Jones in *Our Mutual Friend* on the

penny-pinching Priest, ensuring the Miser of Blewbury a fame that even his hidden millions couldn't buy.

X

The Right Reverend and Right Honourable Frederick Hervey, Earl of Bristol, Bishop of Derry (1730–1803)

'When God created the human race, he made men, women and Herveys'

When an entire family is the subject of an aphorism by Voltaire, it is fair to assume that one might find a number of eccentrics lurking in the family tree. In the case of the Hervey family, this would be something of an understatement, with Frederick, who was simultaneously Earl of Bristol and Bishop of Derry, standing out in a field of strong competition. The Hervey males spent the eighteenth century rampaging around Europe sleeping with anyone they could find. The conquest of successive flowers of European virginity by members of the family became so notorious that it prompted Voltaire to come up with his celebrated maxim. Frederick was the son of Lord John Hervey, a man who bedded both George II's daughter Princess Caroline and his son Frederick, Prince of Wales.

Frederick Hervey was the promiscuous peer's third son and, while his eldest brother was destined for a career in the diplomatic service and the next eldest for a life in the navy, Frederick was selected to pursue a career in the Church. Ordained in 1754, Hervey almost immediately embarked on the Grand Tour of Europe, where he picked

up numerous priceless pieces of art and, despite his clerical status, continued the family tradition of regular and rambunctious continental bonking (to such an extent that he earned the nickname 'the English Casanova'). However, in 1767 he was called back from Europe as his elder brother, who had just been appointed Lord Lieutenant of Ireland, had arranged for him to be made Bishop of Cloyne.

Hervey was not exactly an obvious choice for a senior position of ecclesiastical governance. Aside from his impressive libido, there was also the slight issue of his self-declared agnosticism with regard to the existence of God. Despite these drawbacks, he was eventually confirmed as Bishop and, although the huge amounts of money he was able to throw at the diocese were appreciated, attending to religious matters was further down his list of priorities. One contemporary summed him up thus: 'He is like a shallow stream – rapid, noisy and compelling, but completely useless.'

Hervey much preferred playing games to running his diocese – he was particularly fond of leapfrog and would routinely arrange his Chaplains on the lawn of his palace in such a way as to create a course round which he could jump. It was during one of these innocent adult male outdoor leapfrog sessions in 1768 that he was informed that his brother had secured him promotion again, this time to the Bishopric of Derry. It is said that the Bishop abruptly stopped the game and, with a great shout declaimed, 'Gentlemen, I have outjumped you all! I have leapt from Coyne to Derry!'

Hervey's promotion was considered a bizarre move even at the time; no less a figure than King George III questioned the wisdom of further indulging 'that wicked Prelate'. The advancement of his career did nothing to stop Hervey's

odd behaviour. Indeed, with more clergy under his direct control with whom to have fun, he had, if anything, more opportunities than ever before. He decided to which of his Curates he would give preferment by making them take part in a naked running race around the walls of the city, to the delight of its citizens. On another occasion, he invited the fattest clergy he could find in the diocese to his newly built palace at Downhill and, after feeding them an enormously rich meal, informed them that he would promote the cleric who succeeded in completing an assault course through the bogs of the estate. Hervey was said to be helpless with laughter as he watched the corpulent clergymen struggle through the mire in the hope of securing a plum preferment.

Given his treatment of his clergy, they were probably overjoyed when, having inherited the title Earl of Bristol (and its associated fortune) from his childless elder brother in 1779, Hervey set off on another spree to continental Europe. If the warm air of Italy was supposed to promote lassitude in the boisterous Bishop, it failed. Hervey took advantage of his status by dressing in the flowing robes and gold chains of a Roman Catholic Bishop, which infuriated the local population when they discovered that he was, in fact, an Anglican. On top of this, Hervey provoked the ire of the devoutly Roman Catholic Italians still further in another incident indicative of the sort of 'abominable' behaviour that so scandalised contemporaries. While he was dining in an upper room one evening, Hervey heard the faint sound of chanting and, rushing to the window, observed that a large religious procession, carrying the consecrated Sacrament, was making its way down the narrow street by his lodging. Hervey turned back to the table and, picking up the large bowl of spaghetti that was

the centrepiece of the meal, proceeded to throw the pasta and its attendant sauces over the heads of the congregation below. By the time he reached Rome his reputation was so bad that the Pope personally blocked his attempts to purchase an entire Roman temple to be shipped back to Ireland, despite the Bishop's promise to pay any sum that the authorities named.

In the end – ironically for a man with religious beliefs like Hervey's – it was his role as an Anglican Bishop that led to his eventual demise. For the final thirteen years of his life Harvey didn't once set foot in his diocese, instead gallivanting round Europe bent on the procurement of fine art and the propagation of further pasta-related mayhem. Regrettably for Hervey, his reputation preceded him and, during the French Revolutionary Wars, he was arrested for espionage and imprisoned for nearly two years. On his release, he once more headed for Italy in the hope that the weather would be better and that the Italians had forgotten his previous mischief, making his way towards Rome in 1803. He was sadly mistaken on both counts and died in a cowshed on the outskirts of Rome during a thunderstorm, after the peasant couple with whom he had tried to lodge had refused to allow a Protestant to stay in their house.

Despite his foreign adventures, Hervey's death was much mourned in Ireland, especially by Roman Catholics who had appreciated his manifest failure to enforce any of the punitive restrictions on them that he was supposed to. In a gesture of affection, they raised money to help pay for a memorial at his family seat in Suffolk, where his body was eventually buried after its repatriation from Italy (where it had been kept, as per Hervey's dying wish, in an enormous cask of the very finest sherry). This final flourish of excess by the eccentric Earl-Bishop prompted jokes (of which the

man himself would almost certainly have approved) that the Prelate's greatest success was gifting the world the only known barrel of absolutely authentic 'Bristol' Cream.

ΝUΤΤΥ PROFESSORS

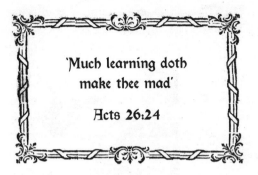

'Much learning doth
make thee mad'

Acts 26:24

The world of academia is an indisputably strange one. If one spends prolonged periods of time dealing with theories, it is perhaps inevitable that the actual skills required for the practice of life become a little rusty. When this general intellectual disengagement is combined with clerical otherworldliness, then a peculiar type of creature is born. Those clergy who spent their careers not only in the public practice of religion but also in pursuit of often staggeringly arcane intellectual goals are the subjects of this chapter.

It will be noted that a sizeable proportion of these idiosyncratic individuals have links to the universities of Oxford and Cambridge. These ancient institutions were both founded with the explicit aim of training clergy for the English Church. Given that both universities owe their very existence to the Church, it is hardly surprising that they have strong clerical traditions to this day. They are, for all their vaunted academic success, eminently strange places. Their colleges are fortress-like structures where teaching, eating, drinking, fighting, fornicating, indeed just about anything you can think of, all take place on top of one another. They have their own recondite traditions, in dress and in behaviour. They run on vast feasts washed down by wine from some of the finest cellars in the Western world. It is no surprise that these incubators of intellect should produce a steady stream of figures for whom the 'real world' is as familiar as the surface of Mars. Both universities are replete with tales of weird and wacky dons – from the history fellow who insisted on giving his tutorials while wedged in his bath to the academic who used to mark his place in library books with bacon sandwiches. The single-minded pursuit of academic brilliance, combined with the unique environment of college life, is a combination that produces some of the most thoroughgoing eccentrics on record. That said, it should be remembered that, for most of their history, Oxford and Cambridge were not the academic hothouses they aspire to be today; they were more a holding pen for the nation's gilded youth and, crucially, the only place where an individual could train for Holy Orders. There were, undoubtedly, a number of figures who lost whole years in libraries, but there were just as many who lost whole years in libation as well.

That said, both universities are now engaged in the dual (and inherently interlinked) processes of modernisation and monetisation. If the world of vintages and Virgil is forever to give way to political concerns and plywood furniture, then Oxbridge's celebrated eccentrics may find themselves squeezed out from their natural habitat by a brave new generation of management consultants. Yet the oddballs of Oxford and characters of Cambridge, lay and ordained, have not breathed their last just yet and, if one visits either university, it is still possible to see, wandering about in an air of dazed confusion at the very concept of reality, the heirs to the tradition of academic strangeness detailed in this section. As for the clergy of this section, some remained in that rarefied university environment to vandalise foliage or rifle through ashtrays, while others took their high-minded eccentricity out with them to be inflicted on unfortunate parishioners, producing tomes on subjects as diverse as werewolves and pornographic plants. A certain type of ageing firebrand would maintain that the pursuit of knowledge and the life of faith are inherently at odds but, if the lives of the following show anything, dear reader, it is that they are both as odd as each other.

I

The Very Reverend Samuel Smith, Dean of Christ Church, Oxford (1765–1841)

'Presence of Mind Smith'

Samuel Smith has the unfortunate distinction of being one of the least successful figures in the history of British academia, lurching from one episode of mismanagement and misadventure to the next. He managed to incur the wrath of his students, fellows and even the Duke of Wellington through his apparently magnetic attraction to disaster. The Deanery of Christ Church has long been considered one of the most prestigious appointments in both the University of Oxford and the Church of England (indeed, today the Dean is the highest paid cleric in the country, earning more than the Archbishop of Canterbury) and many Deans have gone on to hold key Bishoprics and professorships. Smith, by contrast, after a rocky seven years at the helm, arranged to be given a minor Canon's role in Durham, in order to get as far away from Oxford as possible.

Smith had not always been a disastrous figure. The son of the cleric-headmaster of Westminster School, he had a successful university career at Oxford, took Holy Orders and went on to a series of high-profile jobs, including Chaplain to the Speaker of the House of Commons. It was through his political links that he was nominated to run one of Oxford's most prestigious colleges. The prime minister, Lord Liverpool, was concerned by reports that standards of behaviour had slipped beyond even the very low standards expected at that university. Oxford now presents itself as a world leader in education, research and existential angst; in the early 1800s it was nothing of the sort. Essentially a large playground for trainee clergy and young aristocrats to drink in, Oxford was a city of light workloads and heavy hangovers; the historian Edward Gibbon summed up his (not atypical) experience of Magdalen College as 'the most idle and unprofitable fourteen months of my life'.

It was to this centre of decadence that Smith was sent as a sort of academic 'bad cop'. It wasn't long before he had a chance to flex his disciplinary muscles when a student was caught, drunk, having broken out of college after curfew. The undergraduate had a reputation for poor behaviour (having recently been responsible for painting every door in the college's front quad – including the Dean's – bright red) and so Smith had him rusticated for a year. Unfortunately for Smith, the student in question was Lord Charles Wellesley, second son of the victor of Waterloo, the Duke of Wellington. Wellington was furious at what he saw as Smith's overreaction, and immediately removed his son from the college altogether, pointedly sending him to the rival Trinity College in Cambridge instead.

As if losing a notable pupil and irritating a national hero wasn't a bad enough start, Smith took no time at all in blotting his copybook yet further. At a loss for something to do one day, Smith and a friend decided to take what was supposed to be a relaxing boat trip down the River Isis from Oxford to Radley, a few miles downstream. Some hours after leaving, Smith returned wet-trousered to college, where someone enquired as to his companion. Smith replied that they had managed to spring a leak and, in their clumsy attempts to bail out the sinking craft, his friend fell into the water and, in his panicked attempts to get back in, was in danger of capsizing the boat. Smith then recounted matter-of-factly, 'neither of us could swim and, if I had not shown great presence of mind and hit him on the head with a boat hook, we might both have drowned'. The farcical incident of the Dean's boat trip led to a new nickname that spread across Oxford: 'Presence of Mind Smith'.

Smith's attempts to impose himself as an authority figure were in tatters before they had even really begun. By 1829, the country and the university were both hugely divided over the issue of Catholic emancipation. The university elected its member of parliament (as it did until 1950), Sir Robert Peel, who was broadly supported by moderate Tory figures such as Smith. Despite his moderate leanings, Peel's long-standing links to Ireland and the policy of the university meant he felt compelled to resign over the Catholic issue and contest the seat in a by-election. Smith was totally unable to control the Canons, fellows or students at Christ Church, who were split between pro- and anti-Peel parties and routinely resorted to violence when debate proved inconclusive. The final straw came when a group of anti-Peel figures vandalised an ancient door in college with the message 'NO PEEL'.

In the end Peel (who Smith had, obviously, backed) lost the election to an ultra-Tory committed to opposing emancipation. Smith's authority had evaporated and he was desperate to resign. Unfortunately, the only person who could provide him with a new appointment was the King on the advice of the prime minister, who happened to be none other than his old foe, the Duke of Wellington. Smith must have been overjoyed when, in 1830, Wellington's government collapsed and he was replaced by Earl Grey. Smith lost no time whatsoever in handing in his resignation to the new administration and taking a quiet job in Durham, showing the 'Presence of Mind' to avoid Oxford unless entirely necessary in his twilight years.

II

The Reverend Thomas Espin,
Vicar of Cow Law (1858–1934)

Red Dwarfs and Rifle Ranges

An individual with a name like Thomas Henry Espinell Compton Espin was bound to be somewhat precocious. The child of a moderately successful clergyman, he was destined to enter Holy Orders as well. However, as a sixteen–year-old schoolboy, the passing of Coggia's Comet (a flaming piece of space rock, visible to the naked eye, that briefly enthralled Victorian Britain) inspired in him a lifelong love of astronomy and of science more generally. While later twentieth-century rhetoric would seek to paint science and faith as irreconcilable enemies, for Espin they were two complementary approaches to the world that took up the vast majority of his life, without any sense of incongruity whatsoever.

After some time spent in France he went to Oxford and, although he was technically meant to be studying theology, spent most of his time helping to build telescopes and observing the stars. He was considered so helpful by the Professor of Astronomy (an enormously overweight clergyman called Charles Pritchard who, when not leading services or eating, pioneered the use of planetary photography) that he was allowed to use the university's brand new telescope. The young Espin's interest did not go unnoticed and, in 1878, aged just nineteen, he was elected to the Royal Astronomical Society. Despite having neglected theology altogether during his Oxford career, he was ordained in 1881 and, after a string of curacies, he found himself installed as Vicar of the small County Durham town of Tow Law.

Tow Law was a small enough parish to provide Espin with the free time to continue astronomising. He originally had to make do with observing the stars through a pair of specially adapted opera glasses. However, after years of building devices and tinkering with lenses, he amassed possibly the most advanced personal observatory in the world. Espin was responsible for the discovery of over 2,500 'double stars' (pairs of stars that appear to orbit each other, from which relative masses can be determined). Perhaps his most important astrological work was his cataloguing of hundreds of 'red stars' (stars that have metal oxides present), work that was crucial in the identification of 'red dwarfs' and 'red giants' some years later, enabling the galaxy to be mapped and dated more effectively.

Espin was not, however, an individual who had his eyes fixed only on the heavens or his head in the clouds. He was adamant that both science and religion could be used to make the lives of ordinary people better and, in Tow Law, that is exactly what they did. He had read, with enormous interest, of the first successful X-ray in 1895 and, the following year, he set out to build his own. He found that his homemade coil batteries were not up to the job and so constructed an enormous electrostatic generator powered by members of the choir. He also used the choristers as guinea pigs for the device, testing it on children who had swallowed coins prior to using it on the parish at large. The device was in operation some twenty years before the local hospital got its hands on it, although even the hardy citizens of the North East were said to have been concerned by the volume and sparks generated by the Vicar's device.

The Vicar of Tow Law was particularly fond of adapting things, and that extended to his own vicarage. He built a complex aquarium for his collection of tropical fish and turned his predecessor's spacious wine cellar into a rifle range where he encouraged the local Scouts to experiment with small-bore firearms. His experiments and adaptations were not always at the risk of his parishioners' health; during a tuberculosis outbreak, he arranged for a well-ventilated sanatorium to be built in the grounds of the vicarage, much to the relief of those afflicted in the parish. He was well regarded by the parish, who indulged their scientist-Vicar, even in his more eccentric moments (such as when he became convinced that he'd disproved Darwin through the discovery of some local fossils). When he died in 1934, he had been Vicar for nearly fifty years – his death was not only mourned in Tow Law but by scientists across the world, including those in the American NACA (the predecessor of

NASA). His X-ray machine was given to the local doctor and his telescope eventually found its way to the University of Newcastle, but only after a rigorous cleaning; his successor as Vicar was not so scientifically minded and had been using the great Priest-scientist's private observatory as a hen house. The discoveries made in this unlikely corner of County Durham were not forgotten – Espin's research continues to be of use to astronomers, and in tribute there is a large crater on the moon named after the eccentric Vicar of Tow Low.

III

The Reverend Dr William Spooner, Warden of New College, Oxford (1844–1930)

Worms, Wordplay and 'a half-warmed fish'

If life were fair, William Spooner would be remembered by a small group of academics for a series of moderately interesting lectures on Aristotle and for his long association with New College, Oxford. However, his long service and philosophical predilections are quite forgotten by the millions of English speakers who owe to him 'the Spoonerism'. Spooner was generally absent-minded but his particular tendency to transpose the initial letters or syllables of pairs of words or phrases (such as when he supposedly fumed that a lazy undergraduate had 'tasted two worms') meant that he fast became famous in Oxford for verbal mix-ups. The transposition of letters obviously predates Spooner (indeed, one of the earliest written examples we have is also from a Priest, albeit a French one; Rabelais deliberately confused his letters to make the French for 'the woman was mad at Mass' become 'the woman has a soft arse'...).* But Spooner was indisputably the master of the form.

William Spooner was born to a relatively ordinary middle-class family in London. He was born albino and accordingly had very poor eyesight (later colleagues would describe him as looking like a strange sort of hunched rabbit, but observed that he had the spirit of a lion). Spooner was clearly a talented child, becoming the first boy not to have previously gone to Winchester School to attend New College, Oxford, when he won a double scholarship there in 1861. He excelled, especially in Greek literature and philosophy, was made a fellow and, in 1875, was ordained Priest and appointed Dean of the college, putting him in charge of leading public worship on a regular basis. In such a role, speaking in front of people is unavoidable and the students at New College supposedly first noticed his peculiar verbal habit when he announced a hymn as 'Kinkering Congs their Titles Take'.

Slowly, Spooner's verbal tic became notorious, and acquired an almost mythical status around Oxford. It did not prevent him from being elected Warden of the College in 1903, perhaps after the college authorities decided to limit his accidental blasphemy in the pulpit (he once referred to God as 'a shoving leopard') and move him to a less onerous sinecure. Inevitably some stories are apocryphal (it is not known, for instance, whether he actually did inform Queen Victoria that he had 'a half-warmed fish in my bosom'), but it is fairly clearly attested that, during the college's celebration of her Diamond Jubilee, he did propose a toast to 'the Queer old Dean'. Eventually, generations of sniggering Oxford undergraduates carried the reputation of Spooner and his 'isms' into the wider world (although Spooner's rare encounters with the general

---

*   *'Femme folle à la Messe/Femme molle à la fesse.'*

public probably helped, for example when he informed a woman who was in the wrong seat at church that her 'pie was occupewed'). They often added invented or half-remembered Spoonerisms of their own and so a new reputation for the funny little Oxford academic was formed.

Fewer people are aware of the extent of Spooner's muddling up in life. When the salt cellar fell over at a college dinner one evening, Spooner promptly poured his entire glass of wine on it (presumably half-remembering that one pours salt onto spilt red wine to prevent staining). He was equally adept at mixing up people, once asking an old member who was visiting the college in the 1920s, 'Was it you who was killed in the Great War or your brother?' Despite his manifest eccentricity, Spooner was well loved in his college and his city. When he finally died, the *Times* obituary observed that, despite his fame as a bungler of words, 'he was never afraid of conversation'. A somewhat bereft New College commissioned a large portrait of the small, rabbit-like man with the speech impediment who had been such a part of college life for over sixty years; it still hangs in their hall in Oxford today.

IV

Canon Frederick Simpson,
Dean of Trinity College, Cambridge (1883–1974)

The Snipper

The son of a Vicar, Simpson originally studied at Queen's College, Oxford, where, having done catastrophically in Latin and Greek, he soon discovered a passion for history. Rather more successful in his history exams, he was ordained and set off for a short curacy in the Lake District. He spent almost no time on parish duties, instead researching and writing the first volume of what was to be a four-volume masterpiece on the life of French Emperor Napoleon III. This first volume was incredibly well received and, in 1911, Simpson was offered a fellowship at Trinity College, Cambridge. There he stayed for the next six and a half decades.

Simpson just about managed to produce the second volume in 1923. However, as a series of less favourable reviews made clear, it was obvious he had lost interest. This was undoubtedly true; the technological advances of the First World War had brought him a much more interesting hobby than the study of the French Second Empire – flight. It was in the early 1920s that Simpson acquired his first plane, a canvas and wood contraption that was considered by others to be manifestly unsafe. Despite this, he managed to persuade a series of young pilots to fly him around (although he had a great love of planes, there is no record of his actually learning to fly). By the 1930s, he had purchased for himself a slightly sturdier Tiger Moth, the model of plane used by the nascent RAF, and would employ amateur pilots to fly him over to France when he got bored with college life.

Despite continued pressure from his peers in the world of academia finally to finish his magnum opus, an ageing Simpson always managed to find an excuse for not doing any work. He feigned an interest in the college gardens; however, it soon became clear that his interest was in fact inclined towards the destruction rather than the cultivation of horticulture. His rooms in the Great Court at Trinity suddenly filled with a veritable selection of secateurs, shears and pruning saws. Simpson would be seen wandering the gardens with cutting implements of varying sizes, pausing to delicately snip or roughly hack off bits of foliage as he saw fit. He never cleared up any of his cuttings, preferring to leave a trail of debris, which invoked the tremendous ire of the college gardeners but did at least have the small advantage of making him traceable if ever he was needed. Such was his predilection for horticultural vandalism that he earned a new nickname: 'Snipper' Simpson.

Despite his refusal to finish his historical work, he did continue to supervise undergraduates in their studies – a favourite pupil of his was the traitorous Cambridge spy Guy Burgess. He was assiduous in his attendance of chapel as well, despite his own occasionally expressed doubts about the Divine nature of Jesus. He only had a small selection of sermons that he tended to preach on a rotational basis, but his eloquence and style of delivery were such that most of the students and fellows didn't especially mind. By the time he died, at the ripe old age of ninety-one, he had become something of a legendary figure in Cambridge, and stories of the hunched figure in a grey scarf either scuttling out of college to be flown over the Channel or leaving a trail of destruction through the gardens still enliven the monotony of high-table conversation to this day.

V

The Reverend Professor Stephen Reay, Laudian Professor of Arabic at Oxford (1782–1861)

Lost in the Library

Stephen Reay is a remarkable figure precisely because he was so *un*remarkable. He managed to attain one of the most prestigious professorial chairs at the University of Oxford despite having produced only one publication in his entire life, and that only a pamphlet. Having attained it, he spent the rest of his career getting lost in libraries and pretending to be deaf.

Reay was born in Montrose where his father was Vicar to a small congregation of English worshippers who, for reasons both social and doctrinal, refused to worship with their Scottish neighbours in the Presbyterian church there. He went first to Edinburgh to study philosophy and mathematics and then on to Chester (where his uncle had some influence) to be ordained Priest. After a few years bumbling around assisting his uncle, he eventually popped over the border to Lancashire and became Vicar of the small quarrying town of Haslingden, halfway between Blackburn and Rochdale. This was not exactly a prize posting for a young clergyman – Reay's predecessor, when asked about his parish, had simply quoted Psalm 2, Verse 8: 'I have got the heathen for my inheritance, and the ends of the earth for my possession.'

The heathens of Haslingden might not have had a great appetite for religion, but did manage to provide Reay with a wife, Eleanora, the daughter of the local lord of the manor. With her allowance now supplementing his income, Reay left Lancashire in 1814 and moved to Oxford, where, at the overripe age of thirty-two, he became a student again. He graduated in 1817 and immediately set to work writing a pamphlet defending the Church Missionary Society after its reputation was besmirched in a speech made by the Archdeacon of Bath. Reay's pamphlet did not exactly flatter the Archdeacon and so he had it published under a pseudonym, 'Pileus Quadratus', which, although it sounds like it might be something to do with haemorrhoids, actually translates from the Latin as Mr Square Hat, a name Reay thought side-splittingly hilarious.

Failings of humour aside, Reay's pamphlet caught the attention of prominent evangelicals in the university. Oxford historically was (and, broadly, still is) a predominantly High Church city and so evangelical talent tended to be somewhat thin on the ground. As a result of a lack of other Low Church candidates, Reay was almost immediately installed as Vice-Principal of St Alban Hall, a tiny subsidiary of Merton College, the socially parched but academically rigorous headquarters of Oxford evangelicalism. Reay caught the attention of the exceptionally named Reverend Dr Bulkeley Bandinel. Bandinel, who resembled a basset hound, was the long-serving chief librarian of the Bodleian, the university's central holding library. With the expansion of the University Press (and the rigid adherence to the rule that the Bodleian had to hold a copy of every book produced there, regardless of its relevance) as well as his own predilection for acquiring rare manuscripts, Bandinel found he needed an assistant and, in 1828, appointed Reay.

Because he had some knowledge of Hebrew, Reay was put in charge of the library's enormous Oriental Manuscript collection which, thanks to Bandinel's compulsive purchasing, numbered thousands of texts in all manner of languages, from Sanskrit to Japanese. According to colleagues, the short-sighted Reay spent most of his time misplacing his glasses and then having to wander through the Bodleian's long corridors to find them again. The library is notoriously cold in the winter and so another pastime of Reay's was to amble around searching for hot air gratings by which he could warm himself. When, in 1840, the university's professorship of Arabic became vacant, Reay was swiftly appointed due to his experience in the Bodleian's Oriental wing.

Despite his prominent position, Reay failed to publish a single work during his twenty-one-year tenure. Unusually for a professor, he refused to take a college position (perhaps because the professorship was historically linked to the heavy drinking, High Church St John's College) and remained pottering round the library. A damp squib in academic terms, Reay was widely respected in Oxford for his charity and kindness. If ever a conversation turned to a subject he did not like or did not understand, he would feign deafness rather than cause social embarrassment. His beloved and long-suffering wife died at the start of February 1861 and, two and a half weeks later, Reay followed her. The strange Scotsman who wandered the Bodleian and who 'never uttered an unkind word of anybody' was laid to rest with his wife at the cemetery of St Sepulchre in Oxford, where their tomb is to this day.

VI

The Reverend Richard Polwhele, Rector of Manaccan (1760–1838)

The Polemicist Parson

Richard Polwhele was a man with a great many opinions on a great many subjects, almost all of them unfavourable. From Methodism and marriage to botany and bosoms, the Rector of Manaccan would write to anybody about anything. Indeed, he published two volumes of work with the worryingly vague title *Discourses on Different Subjects* where he wrote, at length, about his opinions on various unrelated matters. His literary output was enormous, but he was perhaps most noted for a bizarre poem in which he put forward his rather unique theory that studying plants was as bad as, if not worse than, looking at pornography.

Polwhele was born in a tiny hamlet outside Truro to an impoverished member of the local gentry. He was a precocious child who showed a predilection for local history and poetry, with a teenage fixation on Druids. He eventually went to Oxford with the initial intention of taking a course in law. However, perhaps due to his chronic inability to focus on a single subject, he left without receiving a degree and joined the Church instead. After a brief trip back to Cornwall, he eventually became Curate of Kenton near Exeter. There he spent most of his time convening 'literary societies' with other gentlemen of leisure where they spent prolonged periods of time reciting their own poetry – how his parish fared is not recorded. One group that met, conveniently, at the Globe pub in Exeter, even went so far to publish a collection of their works and elected Polwhele as editor, who promptly filled it with large sections of his own work. When he suggested that he edit a second edition, he was booted out of the club and out of the county.

By 1794, Polwhele returned to Cornwall and the tiny parish of Manaccan. He had begun to write a mammoth history of Devon, financed by public subscription. However, the affair at Exeter and the incredibly poor quality of the first volume led his readers to demand their money back. Despite monetary difficulties, he continued to write vociferously and viciously. A particular target of his ire was the author and feminist Mary Wollstonecraft. In 'The Unsex'd Female' he portrayed her as a satanic figure, leading the female literati astray with her dangerous ideas, among which he afforded pride of place to the study of plants. Botany appears to have horrified Polwhele, with the poem containing quasi-erotic imagery of women's bosoms heaving over what would now be considered biology fieldwork. He had a particular distaste for the lily, the 'organ' of which he felt demonstrated an 'unhallowed lust'.

As well as his broadsides against flowers, Polwhele published several polemical attacks on the Methodists (of which there were huge numbers in Cornwall at the time). However, Polwhele was not exclusively a rabid polemicist. After the sorry story of his history of Devon, he turned his attention to his native county. His history of Cornwall was much more successful and is still referred to this day, not least because his sloppy editing of primary sources provides convincing evidence that the Cornish language survived in spoken form for some years longer than was previously thought. Eventually, in 1838, worn out by the continued existence of both Methodism and mammaries, Polwhele died in Truro, near his birthplace, arguably the only place he really belonged.

VII

The Reverend Francis Hugh Maycock,
Principal of Pusey House (1903–80)

Naps and Nicotine – the Laid-back Life
of Oxford's Favourite Uncle

Pusey House is part church, part library, part hall of residence in the middle of Oxford. It was set up in the late nineteenth century when paranoid clergy were adamant that the attacks on the Irish Church by the Liberal party would inevitably lead to the secularisation of the university and the disestablishment of the Church. Of course, no such thing happened – the colleges kept their chapels and so Pusey House had to reinvent itself. It found a role as an unabashed celebration of all things High Church. From keeping bundles of letters from Catholic turncoat Cardinal Newman (which were, until recently, regularly hidden under jumpers and stolen by devout Roman Catholic clergy as secondary relics) to displaying the death mask of the great Oxford Movement cleric E. B. Pusey during post-service sherry, Pusey House still provides Oxford with theological scholarship, impressive music and liturgy. and just a soupçon of madness to this day.

Such an institution has, unsurprisingly, attracted its fair share of eccentric leaders, from the redoubtable Vincent Stuckey Stratton Coles, a large man who used to sit on people who expressed sympathy for the Parliamentarian side in the English Civil War, to Cheslyn Jones, a Welsh narcoleptic who wrapped the chapel's main paschal candle in barbed wire and had a penchant for Rich Tea biscuits dipped in sherry. However, perhaps the most interesting figure to lead this centre of piety and learning was the Reverend Francis Hugh Maycock, known around Oxford simply as 'Uncle Hugh'. Maycock had been educated at Tonbridge School where he had played cricket but not done much else. From there he went to Christ Church, Oxford, where, as he recounted in later years, one of his more eccentric tutors became convinced that he was turning into a mushroom. Uncle Hugh therefore succeeded in getting an impressively low third-class history degree. Thinking he'd try his hand at theology instead, he changed tack, only to manage an even lower third. He took Holy Orders and, after a short curacy, went out to Malawi as a missionary.

While in Malawi, he managed to get bitten by a tsetse fly which resulted in him being perpetually sleepy for the rest of his life. He would sometimes sleep for eighteen hours a day, once telling an undergraduate who had asked him how he ordered his schedule, 'when I wake up in my pyjamas, I know it's time for Mass; when I wake up in my trousers, I know it's time for tea'. After returning to England, he became Vicar of Little St Mary's in Cambridge, a bastion of 'smells and bells' Anglo-Catholicism in Low Church East Anglia. After seven years in Cambridge he was offered, despite his less than glittering academic record, the post of Principal of Pusey House and so Uncle Hugh gathered up his catering pack of cigarettes (he was a notorious chainsmoker) and his collection of antique pawnbroker's balls (his other hobby aside from smoking – he claimed to have some that had belonged to the Medici) and returned to Oxford.

Uncle Hugh was an immediate success at Pusey. Renowned for his geniality and his ability to listen, it was often difficult to find him in his study, which became within weeks an almighty muddle of books and papers piled to the ceiling, all enveloped by a dense cloud of cigarette smoke. His detachment became famous in Oxford, a town where people are often wont to invest heavily in matters that aren't of the least importance. Indeed, he is only ever recorded as becoming animated once – when a particularly long croquet game disturbed one of his naps. This detachment meant he was in great demand as a listener. It was said that when students would come and pour their hearts out at Uncle Hugh's feet, by the time they were done they would find that their troubles had dissolved into the great cloud of burning tobacco. He also became known for his pithy advice, counselling one young man that true maturity was 'seeing the truth in platitudes'.

Alongside his near constant napping and his enthusiasm for pawnbroking memorabilia, Oxford provided other outlets for Uncle Hugh's eccentricities; he would drive groups of students to his favourite pubs in the countryside surrounding the city, hurtling along at great speed wearing a First World War flying helmet that he had procured. He particularly enjoyed having American passengers as it meant he had an excuse to drive on the right-hand side of the road, scattering petrified motorists as he did so.

By 1970, Uncle Hugh retired and went to be Chaplain to an order of nuns down the road from Oxford in Burwash, where ten years later he died. Unfortunately, he managed to outlive quite comfortably his successor at Pusey, who died almost immediately after taking the Principal's post when he fell off a ladder trying to fit a lightbulb. Uncle Hugh, when approached for comment by the press, observed in his characteristic, dispassionate way that the incident had caused some 'unfortunate confusion', before returning to the nunnery for a well-earned rest.

VIII

The Reverend Dr Vicesimus Knox, Headmaster of Tonbridge School (1752–1821)

The Pacifist Pedagogue

During the eighteenth and nineteenth centuries, the cleric-headmaster was not an unusual figure. With the Church responsible for almost all education in the country, from Sunday Schools up to the universities, clergy found themselves in charge of educational establishments both great and small. In many ways, Vicesimus Knox was one of the greatest of this unique breed – he was a runaway success in terms of expanding his school and his pedagogical views were praised by such notable literary figures as Jane Austen and Dr Johnson. However, Knox was a not uncontroversial figure. Whether through his hugely unpopular attempts to preach pacifism to a nation embroiled in the Napoleonic Wars or his strange beliefs about the effects of reading novels, he invariably expended any credit he had built up through his scholarship by championing unpopular causes.

Knox was born in Newington, then a village near London. His father was also a clergyman-headmaster and also called Vicesimus. The unusual name is Latin for twentieth, although neither father nor son was the twentieth child; it appears to have simply been a slightly bizarre family tradition. (Knox did not continue this with his own son, giving him the slightly more prosaic name Thomas.) In 1771 he went to St John's College, Oxford, and, five years later, was made a fellow and took Holy Orders. However, his tenure was rather short-lived as in 1778 his father's ill health meant that, aged just twenty-six, he had to take over as headmaster at Tonbridge.

His father had not left the school in the best of situations – there were only twenty pupils left by the time Vicesimus the Younger arrived to start work. However, through good investments, marketing and his own reputation as a skilled preacher, within a few years there were more than eighty. Knox capitalised on his reputation by editing and publishing an abridged anthology of famous poems and prose – he was of the firm opinion that most things could be skim-read and quoted from, opining that 'it often happens that quotations constitute the most valuable part of a book'.

The anthology was a huge success, becoming a standard in most libraries across the country, even earning Knox a mention in Jane Austen's *Emma*. The anthology made up for Knox's previous foray into publication – a collection of essays which included a tirade against the reading of novels. Knox believed that the publication of novels was indicative of the 'degeneracy of the present age', and that reading them not only distracted young men from their education but also encouraged them towards masturbation, 'the solitary vice'.

By the early 1790s, Knox's successes at Tonbridge and as a published author had made him a household name, much in demand as a speaker and preacher. However, by this point Britain was engaged in a brutal war against revolutionary France. Knox felt moved by his reading of the Gospel to oppose the war publicly and instead urge the government to work towards 'the total abolition of war and the establishment of perpetual and universal peace'. Such sentiments may not seem unusual coming from a clergyman in public life today but in fiercely patriotic Georgian England, with a bloodthirsty regime undertaking the wholesale slaughter of its own populace just across the Channel, Knox's preaching of peace was enormously controversial. In the summer of 1794, he had been asked to preach to a fashionable society crowd in Brighton and chose as his subject 'The Unlawfulness of Offensive War'. Having preached a particularly strongly pacifist sermon, rumour circulated in Brighton that the headmaster was a traitor. Some days later, a group of off-duty soldiers recognised Knox in a theatre and began heckling him, stirring up their fellow theatregoers against the erstwhile cleric. Eventually, the mob became so violent that Knox had to flee by the stage door, only just escaping with his life.

The Brighton incident ruined Knox's reputation. Parents began to withdraw their children from his school, fearful of what he might be teaching there, and Knox had to take on a series of jobs in churches around Tonbridge in order to maintain his income. He didn't exactly help his position by publishing a book the following year accusing the government of despotism under the cover of the war effort. What had once been considered eloquence and charm was now decried as vulgar and showy. It is a mark of how little authority he had left that he failed to put down a number of near riots by the pupils at the school. Eventually, in 1812, Knox handed over the headmastership to his son and, nine years later, his spirit broken standing up for his principles, he died.

IX

Canon Claude Jenkins, Canon of Christ Church and Regius Professor of Ecclesiastical History at Oxford (1877–1959)

Dr Claude – Unkempt Genius and Food Thief

One would be hard-pressed to find a nuttier professor than Canon Claude Jenkins, for twenty-five years the Professor of the History of the Church at the University of Oxford. The epitome of academic eccentricity, he amused and terrified his students in equal measure with his erratic behaviour. Slovenly, forgetful and almost always covered in fragments of his last meal, Jenkins was also widely considered to be one of the great scholars of his generation.

After his own time at university, he took Holy Orders

and, when it became clear that he was temperamentally unsuited to anything but academic work, was made the Archbishop of Canterbury's personal librarian in 1910. During his time at Lambeth Palace he had the foresight to move a number of valuable tomes out of London when it became clear that it would be the target of German air raids in the First World War. Although he saved the books from the devastation wrought by Zeppelins, he forgot to inform anyone about his plans, leading to successive bemused Archbishops of Canterbury having to field queries on the whereabouts of documents of historic importance (such as the original diaries of Prime Minister William Gladstone) only to be informed that Jenkins had secreted them sixty miles away in a cellar at Christ Church in Oxford.

It was to Christ Church that Jenkins (who had kept up an impressive publishing output during his time as librarian) was appointed in 1934, when he took the Regius Professorship of the History of the Church. The role came with a number of privileges but also, more worryingly for the haphazard Jenkins, responsibilities. One of his obligations was to deliver a lecture series on the history of the Early Church to undergraduates sitting for theology degrees. Rather than split these up, Jenkins decided to give a number of these consecutively, attaching a large alarm clock to a string around his neck, the ringing of which served as a reminder to change subject. He was occasionally called to fulfil clerical duties at the cathedral which adjoins the college, while his impressive voice was considered a highlight of evensong; he was less adept at other services, however, and tried to avoid doing them altogether. He never conducted marriages (matrimony was one of the two things he claimed to abhor; the other was the domestic cat) and when he was finally cajoled into conducting a christening, after over forty years of ordained ministry, he was confused when the infant was unable to shake his hand.

Jenkins was not, however, just a doddery old professor (although in his mid-fifties he was described as looking 'at least a hundred'). He was notoriously parsimonious, opposing any attempt by the college to sell its assets on the cheap or to spend more than it need. This penny-pinching extended to his housekeeping; he would routinely conceal food from the college's high table in the pockets of his cassock or the folds of his gown to eat at other opportunities. After one dinner, Jenkins lost his footing on the stairs outside hall and tumbled in a flurry of Melba toast that he'd nabbed from the pâté course. He was famed for smoking the most appalling smelling cigarettes which contained a tobacco of his own devising: half-dried beech leaves and half-old cigar butts from the ashtrays of the Senior Common Room.

These two aspects of his lifestyle meant that Jenkins was invariably smeared in food and ash – but scruffiness wasn't limited to his personal dress. The house he had been given in the main Quad at Christ Church was notoriously messy. He employed a housekeeper which seemed to solve the problem until, one day, he arrived late for a college meeting with the explanation that she had unfortunately just died, but that there was no need for concern as he had 'popped her on a kitchen chair where she'll be alright until I return'. From then on, Jenkins' house became a tip. Books towered up to the ceiling, making navigation of the premises only possible through narrow alleyways that would themselves become blocked when a stack collapsed. Even the bath tub was eventually filled with books. Between the dust, books and pieces of half-forgotten, pilfered food, it was often easy to miss Jenkins himself. One undergraduate described going in for a tutorial only to find the house abandoned.

Assured by the porters that Canon Jenkins was in fact present, he returned, to be given the shock of his life when Jenkins emerged from underneath a pile of old newspaper.

By the time he died, Jenkins had become as much a part of Oxford life as the ancient stones of Christ Church itself. Despite his eccentricities he left an impressive academic legacy, supervising a generation of pre-eminent Oxford figures (including Hugh Trevor Roper and W. H. Auden, who wrote a poem to him that ended 'Cherubim sing: all glory, laud,/ eternal honour to Dr Claude!'). He also published a series of books and reviews on ecclesiology still referred to today.

At the reading of his will there were two notable requests that show both his charity and his parsimony. Firstly, he left his enormous library to the poorest, all-female college (ensuring the small population of women students at Oxford had as good access to books as their male counterparts); secondly, no doubt remembering the many stubs of cigars it had given him, he left £100 to keep a permanent supply of tobacco in the Senior Common Room.

X

The Reverend Sabine Baring-Gould, Rector of Lew Trenchard (1834–1924)

The Wannabe Van Helsing Who Inspired Henry Higgins

It hardly needs saying that Sabine Baring-Gould is not a name that crops up in casual conversation a great deal these days. Yet, in Victorian times, the enigmatic incumbent of Lew Trenchard was something of a celebrity. Known throughout the country for writing the words to 'Onward, Christian Soldiers' (a celebrity no doubt consolidated by the jaunty tune composed by Sir Arthur Sullivan, of Gilbert and Sullivan fame), tales of his eccentricities, the scandalous circumstances of his marriage and his well-known interest in the occult ensured him A-list status in late Victorian Britain. He has been put forward by some as a model for Sherlock Holmes (and, indeed, in subsequent Holmes fiction has been described as the great detective's godfather). While today he may be largely forgotten, the air of mystery that he cultivated was like catnip to the Victorian public.

Baring-Gould was born to an ancient family in the depths of Devonshire. His ancestor had been awarded the manor of Lew Trenchard as a reward for his role in the Third Crusade, but by the early nineteenth century a combination of familial restlessness and mounting heating costs inspired Sabine's father to cart his wife and child around Europe on a series of tours. As such, by the time he was a teenager, Sabine's itinerant lifestyle had resulted in fluency in five languages and a serious bronchial disease (the news of which greatly cheered his father as it provided an excuse for further travel). In 1852, he went to Clare College, Cambridge, which he hated, but where he first felt a call towards Holy Orders. His father, horrified by the idea that his son and heir might become a Vicar, talked him out of it and so, after graduating, Sabine became a teacher at Hurstpierpoint College in Sussex.

At Hurstpierpoint he began to show signs of the studied eccentricity that would become his trademark. He painted the windows of his classroom over with lurid scenes taken from Spenser's *Faerie Queene*, imported a pony from Iceland called Bottlebrush, which he would graze on the school playing fields, and insisted on teaching whole lessons with his tame pet bat perched on his shoulder, bravely ploughing on through textbooks even as the animal defecated down his back. (As a respite from teaching, he also liked to design bookcases.) Eventually, the call to Priesthood which he had suppressed some years earlier became too strong and, in 1864, he took Holy Orders, finding a Curate's post in the small industrial town of Horbury Bridge near Wakefield.

A few years after Baring-Gould arrived in Yorkshire, he fell in love with a young girl, Grace Taylor, who worked at the local mill. His Vicar, scandalised by the match and terrified of the potential wrath of Sabine's erratic father, insisted that Grace be given some sort of education before his Curate proposed. Reluctantly Sabine agreed and, when she returned from being tutored by the Vicar's relatives in York, the two married, and would remain together until Grace's death in 1916. Despite initial concerns, the marriage was a fruitful one: they produced fifteen children. Keeping tabs on his offspring proved to be beyond the faculties of the naturally absent-minded Sabine; at one vicarage party some years later he approached a small child, asking, 'And whose little girl are you?', only to be met with floods of tears and the answer 'Why, Daddy, I'm one of yours!' The story of the well-born Curate and the mill girl scandalised some in Victorian society but inspired others – some years later Baring-Gould's friend George Bernard Shaw used the story as inspiration for his play *Pygmalion*.

It was in Yorkshire that Baring-Gould wrote some of his more notable works. 'Onward, Christian Soldiers' was written, according to the author, in about ten minutes, when it was found there were not enough copies of a suitable hymn for the children to sing in their annual parade around the parish. It was also at Horbury Bridge that he wrote his seminal work on werewolves. Obsessed with the folklore of the moors that surrounded his parish, Baring-Gould began to dig deeper into the stories of lycanthropy he had encountered in local tradition and decided to write a comprehensive book on the subject – one that is still consulted by werewolf hunters to this day.

In 1871 he was finally permitted to take over a church of his own and became Vicar of windswept East Mersea on the Essex coast. The parish was perfect for Baring-Gould, replete with ghostly tales of mysterious figures coming in off the sea. His folkloric endeavours received a financial boost when, in 1872, Sabine's overbearing father died and he became squire of Lew Trenchard. The estate afforded him a sizeable income, which he ploughed into various projects, most notably acquiring books so that he could learn languages such as Icelandic and Basque. In 1881, the elderly rector at Lew Trenchard died and so Baring-Gould, as patron of the parish, appointed himself, living out his final years as both squire and parson. He spent his last forty years going around Devon and Cornwall, forcing baffled farmhands to sing to him – resulting in one of the most important collections of English folksong in existence. The agricultural labourers of the West Country were finally safe from these demands for impromptu performances when, in 1924 at the grand old age of ninety, Baring-Gould was finally laid to rest.

BON VIVEURS

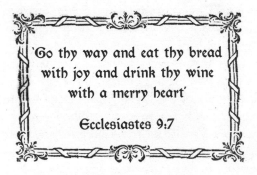

'Go thy way and eat thy bread
with joy and drink thy wine
with a merry heart'

Ecclesiastes 9:7

iven that the central rite of the Christian religion is based around the communal consumption of food and drink, it is hardly surprising that some clergy feel attracted to both. Indeed, the pervading conceptualisation of Heaven found in the Bible and in Church tradition is of an enormous banquet, and many have taken it as no coincidence that the first miracle performed by Christ was the turning of water into wine at the wedding feast at Cana, crucially *after* the revellers were 'well drunk'. An appreciation of the finer things is not limited to life, but might be enjoyed for eternity as well. Of course, when we speak of hedonism in this context we are not dealing with a scone too many at a village fête or sneaking an extra glass of sherry after evensong. Rather, we speak of unabashed gourmands, slathering every meal in double cream and proper, gut-busting boozehounds, who thought nothing of drinking their own bodyweight on a Saturday night before conducting worship a few hours later. The definition of bon viveur employed here is not limited to those who took seriously the biblical command to 'eat and drink' but also those who followed the command to be 'merry'; this chapter contains its fair share of priestly playboys, thrill seekers and mischief makers as well as 'gluttons and winebibbers'.

The clergy in this section are a veritable smorgasbord of characters who, having reconciled themselves to their place in the vale of earthly sorrow, decided to make the best of it and enjoy life to its full. They are only a selection; there was, sadly, no room here for the parson who spent so much time in the saddle that he constructed three hunting lodges in corners of his parish to save him riding all the way home to get a drink, nor the senior Cambridge cleric who was admonished by the Archbishop of Canterbury himself for his bibulous ways, only to die four days into teetotalism. St Irenaeus, an otherwise somewhat stern Bishop in the second century, taught that 'the glory of God is man fully alive', and whether that fullness of life manifested in hours spent gallivanting around the countryside on horseback, chugging vats of brandy, or meticulously planning intricate menus, each of the figures in the section that follows can be said to have followed the Bishop's dictum. While an admirable tradition of asceticism and self-denial is also a part of the Church's historic inheritance, these clergymen show that a full-throttled, calorie-laden, champagne-fuelled bender is just as much in line with the Christian tradition as any monastic rigour.

The author would humbly suggest that one of the reasons we have such an enduring fascination with the particular sort of people who enjoy themselves, regardless of the consequences, is that they invoke a sort of jealousy among those of us who can't quite bring ourselves to be so

unapologetically carefree. These individuals were unen-
cumbered by giving a damn about their waistlines, their
livers, their personal safety or, perhaps most importantly,
what anybody else thought, in the firm belief that still better
things were to come in the hereafter. Consequently they felt
able to have the sort of adventures that common sense ordi-
narily constrains us from indulging in. These, therefore, are
Priests who provoke a certain armchair envy and rectors
whose lack of rectitude we secretly admire. They are, in
short, vicars who enable us to live vicariously through their
rambunctious enjoyment of all that the Good Lord had
blessed them with. Perhaps, even if we are not minded to
follow their example by volume (indeed, professional medical opinion would strongly advise against such a course),
we might at least take to heart something of their carefree
joie de vivre and 'drink our wine with a merry heart'.

I

Canon Brian Dominic Frederick Titus Leo Brindley, Vicar of Holy Trinity, Reading (1931–2001)

High Heels and Haute Cuisine

Brian Brindley was undoubtedly one of the more colourful
figures of the twentieth-century Church of England. Born
in London, his precociousness manifested itself early when
he insisted on adding 'Dominic', 'Titus' and, later, 'Leo' to
his given names of Brian and Frederick. During his time at
Exeter College, Oxford, he was considered to be one of the
finest wits of his generation, rubbing shoulders with the likes

of Alan Bennett, and was once commissioned to produce an entertainment for the official visit of Princess Margaret. Brindley, not one for convention, wrote a seventeenth--century-style masque entitled *Porci ante Margeritam* or 'Swine before a Pearl'. His appetite for mischief was already present at Oxford – in the weighty college suggestions book he drew a large picture of himself adorned in the robes of a Bishop. Ordination was not, however, his first choice of career; he had a stab at being a disc jockey and then a lawyer before finally deciding to take Holy Orders. Not really knowing what to do with such a figure, the Bishop of Oxford appointed him to the role of Vicar of Holy Trinity in Reading, a squat Victorian box on a main road, essentially earmarked for closure.

On his appointment to Holy Trinity, Brindley became something of a magpie and travelled Europe collecting everything from Gothic reliquaries to the Augustus Pugin-designed choir screen of a major cathedral, all of which ended up crammed into the rather unprepossessing church he'd been lumped with. On top of the Vicar's ornament collection, Holy Trinity became known for its outrageously camp liturgy. One service saw Brindley processing round the church holding the consecrated Sacrament while being fanned by ostrich feathers.

The fame of Holy Trinity spread far and wide under Brindley's leadership. He mischievously took out full-page advertisements in national newspapers announcing 'Fast Trains from Paddington' – the inference being that nothing in London could quite match Holy Trinity and its Vicar. Indeed, in many ways he was right. Brindley became an instantly recognisable sight in Reading – he insisted on curling his hair into the style of a Georgian periwig and would wear high heels (which he had hand-painted bright red) under his cassock while doing his weekly shopping at the supermarket.

Food and drink were, alongside religion, the great loves of Brindley's life. He was famed as an excellent cook, contributing a series of calorie-laden recipes to the pages of the *Church Times*. He loved excess and was famously unable to eat even a quiche at a parish lunch without slathering it in double cream in order to, in his own words, 'make it less rich'. This diet was not without its drawbacks; friends related stories after his death of incidents where entire occasions were ruined by the toxic stench unleashed whenever Brindley happened to break wind. Air pollution aside, Brindley proved to be an extraordinarily effective manager, rising to prominence on the Church of England's General Synod (where, needless to say, his post-session drinks parties became legendary). It was this success that ultimately proved to be his downfall: at a time when the Church was hugely divided over its stance on homosexuality (*plus ça change*), Brindley was recorded publicly admitting he was gay.

Conservative figures successfully clamoured for his removal and, a few years later, Brindley settled into life away from the Priesthood and became a Roman Catholic. He moved away from Holy Trinity, settling in Brighton, where he set about turning the interior of his town house into a replica of the Indo-Chinese Banqueting Room of Brighton Pavilion. His love of both fine cuisine and the dramatic stayed with him until the very end – at the Athenaeum Club during the seven-course celebrations for his seventieth birthday, between the drest crab and the boeuf en croûte, Brindley suffered an enormous heart attack and died.

II

The Reverend Nathaniel Rothwell, Rector of Thursford and Great Snoring (1652–1710)

'a loose and scandalous life, much addicted to excessive drinking and filthy talking'

The Church has long had a slightly conflicted relationship with alcohol. Many, from St Paul to the Puritans, warned strongly against the dangers of being 'given to much wine' (1 Timothy 3:8). However, there have long been vigorous defenders of alcohol consumption among the clergy, reasoning that if Jesus was prepared to turn water into wine at Cana then a little tipple here and there can hardly hurt. Nathaniel Rothwell, if he was ever capable of reasoning at all during his thirty-five-year ministry, was firmly of the latter opinion.

Rothwell had been a moderately successful student at St John's College, Cambridge, and, after various college posts and curacies, was eventually appointed to the living of Thursford and Great Snoring in 1690. Aptly named Great Snoring, not much had changed in this part of rural Norfolk since the Black Death of the mid-fourteenth century. However, with the arrival of the Reverend Nathaniel Rothwell, this tranquil and forgotten corner of East Anglia became the playground of the Church of England's most prolific boozer. Whether in an attempt to continue the excesses of student life or out of sheer boredom with his surroundings, Rothwell soon gained a reputation for mammoth drinking sessions and loutish behaviour.

The end of Sunday services was, for Rothwell, merely the starting pistol for a marathon of alcohol consumption. One Sunday, after performing his morning duties, he went straight to the house of one of his accomplices, a local bricklayer of dubious repute, where he stayed until the early hours of Monday morning drinking his signature cocktail (a mix of brandy and mead) until he could not 'stand without assistance'. Rothwell managed to fall into the fireplace and, brandy-soaked as he was, would have set himself alight were it not for the quick thinking of his drinking companions. This brush with danger had no impact on the clergyman's boozing whatsoever. The following year, after a christening, he made his way to Barney, a small hamlet near Thursford, where he drank through the night. He was observed in the early hours of the following morning, looking 'wild' and searching for brandy and sustenance. Later that day he was eventually found by parishioners passed out in a sandpit, finally bringing his epic session to an end.

As his expedition to Barney shows, it was not only Great Snoring and Thursford that served as arenas for the parson's exploits. In 1703, he made his way to the Red Lion Inn in Fakenham where, under the guise of visiting the town on business, he stayed up all night playing cards with the stable hands, drinking brandy and eventually soliciting a number of complaints from those staying there due to his rambunctious singing and dancing. His gargantuan appetite for brandy, mead – indeed any alcohol he could lay his hands on – not only inspired a love of partying in Rothwell, but also made him inclined to indulge in language unbecoming of one in Holy Orders. In 1708, after downing two whole jugs of his favourite strong drink, he loudly swore by the name of God that 'I had never fucked any woman in my life'. He then proceeded to fall off his chair and, on getting up, put his wig on backwards.

Eventually, the hapless congregations of Thursford and Great Snoring had had enough of picking up their

chronically hungover Priest from various neighbouring
locales and so contacted the Bishop. In late 1708, the
Archdeacon opened an investigation into Rothwell's behaviour with the accusation that he was 'unmindful of his
sacred ministry and lived a 'scandalous life, much addicted
to excessive drinking and filthy talking'. More than forty
villagers testified to the Rector's misbehaviour, including
one of those who had helped save him from the fire. The
case was lengthy, but Rothwell did not live to see its con-
clusion. He died, no doubt at least in part due to the twenty
years of brandy and mead that he had poured into himself,
a year and a half later, at fifty-eight.

III

The Reverend Thomas Patten,
Vicar of Seasalter (1683–1764)

The Smuggling Sermoniser of Seasalter

Part of the purpose of the Church of England (at least
in theory) is that it has a presence in every corner of the
country – from Dover to Durham, Penzance to Penrith.
Inevitably, this admirable mission to be present in every
community has shaped the national Church, providing it
with clergy filled with the particular eccentricities of every
region of England. It also means that there are some church
positions that are less, shall we say, immediately desirable
than others. Historically, one such position was the church
of St Alphege at Seasalter on the north Kent coast.

Today it is a residential suburb of artsy, fashionable

Whitstable, but in the eighteenth century it was just about bottom of the list of potential jobs in the whole Church of England. Most of the village, including the original church, had been washed into the sea by a storm in the medieval period, and some might argue that was for the best. It was constantly lashed by the North Sea resulting in a climate that was considered manifestly unhealthy, and the villagers spent their time either drinking themselves into oblivion or smuggling various goods in from the cliffs under the noses of the customs men.

The failure to fill the position was of acute embarrassment to the Archbishop of Canterbury, whose cathedral was only seven miles away. Most clergymen would spend a year there (at the absolute maximum) before begging to be moved on. Thomas Patten, however, was not like most clergymen. Of humble beginnings, his path to ordination is unclear. However, we know he spent some time as a Chaplain to the Royal Navy and, in 1711, accepted the post of Vicar of Seasalter. Patten was not a man who would let a little thing like his parishioners, the law or the Primate of All England spoil his fun, and so he set about devising a number of ways to enjoy himself in what was, on paper, a dreadful position.

Patten was a man of gigantic appetites. He lived quite openly with his mistress, and his love of eating and drinking to excess was common knowledge. Patten would deliberately preach long and dull sermons that would continue until someone in the congregation held up a lemon – a sign that they would buy the Vicar his drinks for the evening. At this point, Patten would finish off the service with impressive alacrity and dash over the road to the Blue Anchor Inn, in order to lay waste to the unfortunate congregant's tab. The Vicar's wiliness didn't only extend to extorting booze out of his parishioners. If he was ever called on to attend an event in Canterbury, he would deliberately wear the scruffiest clothes he could find and, if the Archbishop was present, immediately approach him and demand an increase in pay.

Patten thoroughly enjoyed winding up successive Archbishops, not only by repeatedly demanding more money, but also by regularly referring to himself as 'Bishop of Whitstable' and to his tiny church as a cathedral. When William Wake was Archbishop he went so far as to visit Patten to question him about his episcopal pretensions; when asked if it was true that he'd assumed the title of a Bishop the Vicar replied, 'I shall answer your Grace's question with another: if it were true would you be such a fool as to take any notice?'

Truculent boozehound he may have been, but Thomas Patten was certainly not an idiot. He found the perfect position to indulge his interests when he got involved with the smuggling operations in the village. The Seasalter Company was a group of smugglers who, in return for Patten informing them about the movements of the authorities, kept the vicarage well stocked with fine French wine, brandy and contraband tobacco. Patten was not above getting his own hands dirty – he tricked a rival group of smugglers into being caught by the Customs men when they failed to cut him in.

Alongside his hobbies of drinking, smuggling and provoking his employer, Patten amused himself by using his parish registers to record his real views of the parishioners he was supposed to be marrying, burying or baptising. Usually parish registers are interminably dull and legalistic, but Patten's gruff wit and (possibly brandy-induced) lack of self-censorship turned those of Seasalter into works of art. He recorded one wedding couple as being 'a gape-mouthed lazy fellow' and 'an old toothless hag' respectively; Elizabeth Johnson was described as 'daughter of the Devil's vice-regent, commonly called the bailiff'; and a young groom's occupation was recorded as 'huntsman to the ancient corporation of cuckolds'. However, he could, in his own way, be kind. When he decided to replace his disintegrating and moth-addled wig, he ordered a new one from a local wig maker and, to celebrate the deal, had dinner with the tradesman. After an inordinate amount of ale had been drunk, Patten thanked the man and promptly cancelled the order he had just put in. Confused by this volte-face, the wig maker demanded an explanation and so Patten confessed that he had, over supper, grown to like the man and so, given that he had no intention of paying for the wig once it was made, felt he should take his swindling elsewhere.

Patten undoubtedly lived life to the full and, where others had failed to make a life worth living in Seasalter, he quite evidently succeeded, remaining Vicar there for fifty-three years (although that may have had something to do with successive Archbishops refusing to give him any other job). For all his rudeness, the parishioners grew to love their drunken smuggler of a parson and, when he died at the age of eighty, commissioned a memorial for him which can still be seen at his 'cathedral' to this day.

IV

The Reverend John 'Mad Jack' Allington, Rector of Barford (1795–1863)

The Mad Vicar of Old Letchworth

Few things have caused the Church of England more internal difficulties in modern times than the subject of sex.

Figures on all sides of the debate have spent hours quoting scripture, exegesis and historic precedents at one another in the vain hope that they might convince the other side. However, in their desire to put forward historical examples, contemporary clergy have arguably missed a key figure: the Reverend John Allington, a leopard-skin-clad cleric who preached a brandy-fuelled gospel of free love in, of all places, Hertfordshire, some 150 years prior to the sexual revolution of the 1960s. Allington, known as 'Mad Jack' or 'the Mad Vicar of Old Letchworth', is one of the most erratic and outrageous figures in the Church's history.

Allington's childhood was comparatively ordinary. The only surviving son of the lord of the manor of Old Letchworth in Hertfordshire, he attended Oxford and was made Deacon in 1819. He immediately took on the role of Rector of Little Barford near Cambridge; however, he almost never visited the parish as most of his time was spent running his estate near Letchworth. In a show of feudal deference, the Vicar of Old Letchworth asked whether Allington might like to take the occasional service given that he was ordained and regularly in the area. The Vicar almost immediately regretted this offer as Allington proceeded to insist on conducting every marriage and christening scheduled to take place, leaving the incumbent the unenviable task of only doing funerals. Eventually, news reached the Vicar of what Allington had been doing in his absence: he routinely replaced readings from the Bible with passages from erotic poems and, instead of extolling the virtues of married life in his wedding sermons, would instead preach paeans to the idea of free love. Feeling that the lord of the manor had pushed things too far, the Vicar complained to the Bishop, and Allington was suspended from preaching.

Allington did not take this well. He converted part of his ancestral home, Letchworth Hall, into a chapel and set up his own church in direct defiance of the Bishop. Allington's services were far from conventional. Firstly, the main incentive for people to come was the unlimited beer and brandy that Allington offered before, during and after the service, resulting in something more than a casual pre-prandial tipsiness from a post-Mass sherry. This free alcohol attracted a large number of waifs and strays from the surrounding area, including a large group of gypsies who camped nearby and became the most dedicated parishioners of the man they called 'the Parson gone out of business'.

After his bizarre congregation had gathered, Allington would begin proceedings by playing a voluntary on the broken-down piano that he christened 'Tidlee Bump'. He would then 'do the rounds' of the congregation. When he was sober enough, this meant riding a hobby horse (an early form of bicycle) up and down the aisle until he fell off, to the great amusement of those present. When he had slightly overindulged in the pre-service brandy, he would career up and down, sitting in a wheelbarrow propelled by his servants. Allington would then change into his 'vestments', which consisted of an old leopard skin and a pair of Moroccan slippers, and proceed to give a reading from whichever love poem took his fancy. He would then climb up into his 'pulpit' (a hollowed-out tree trunk) and proceed to preach a sermon on his favourite subject, the merits of free love. When he had grown bored, he would signal the end of the service by taking off his wig and throwing it into the inebriated crowd. He would then play a final hymn on a pair of music boxes, accompanied by a group of gypsy violinists whom he would 'conduct' using the mangy tail of the leopard skin.

As if the total insanity of his professional life were not enough, Allington proved to be as egregiously eccentric in private. He had a large lake commissioned in the grounds of the Hall which was modelled on a map of the oceans of the world. Allington would invite guests to hear him lecture on geography (a subject about which he knew next to nothing) while he manoeuvred himself around the lake in a punt. A punt was not his most eccentric mode of transport – he went through a period of insisting on being carried around in a coffin by the servants, popping his head up to greet horrified parishioners as he went. Mad Jack's eccentricity (coupled with his love of fine brandy) proved to be his undoing. In 1863 he fell ill and for three days refused any form of treatment, instead forcing his long-suffering servants to take whatever unpleasant tonics and tinctures his doctor prescribed. Intractable to the bitter end, he eventually decided to administer his own prescription, which was, predictably, a large tumbler of cognac. The Mad Vicar of Old Letchworth eagerly gulped down his self-prescribed medicine and, to the surprise of nobody present, immediately dropped down dead.

V

The Reverend James Woodforde, Vicar of Weston Longville (1740–1803)

The Father of Food Blogging

A diary is an immensely personal thing, and there are many ways in which individuals throughout history have chosen to put pen to paper in order to mark the ups and downs of their daily lives. The pages of Samuel Pepys are filled with court intrigue; Franz Kafka's with sexual frustration and existential angst. The notebooks filled by the Reverend James Woodforde, however, are filled with pages and pages of menus. More than two centuries before people became obsessed with recording their meals on Instagram, James Woodforde was recording every morsel (and there were many) that he had plated up in front of him. He was the original food blogger par excellence. Woodforde was a Somerset clergyman's son and, when he went up to Oriel College, Oxford, in 1758, his father advised that he keep a small book of all his expenditure. The young Woodforde duly obliged and, over the next forty-five years, this trivial accounting exercise became the sumptuous record book of a true bon viveur, replete with asides by the author detailing the mundane realities of life in the late eighteenth century.

Woodforde's love of fine wine and food clearly began early. His Oxford years are a record of the enormous quantities of alcohol drunk and meat eaten by him and his peers. In one entry, Woodforde records how a fellow student bet a small amount of money that he could write out a sentence from the Bible after consuming three bottles of port, wryly following up that, after two and a half bottles, the young scholar was barely able to stand and speak let alone write, and so the bet was considered forfeit. Woodforde himself was sometimes on the receiving end of the more boisterous challenges of his fellow students; the evening of his graduation he describes drinking a gargantuan amount of claret and port and crawling into bed, only to be hauled out some hours later by his equally inebriated fellows and forced to ride all the way to neighbouring Abingdon with them to try to find an open inn.

Woodforde left the college to work as Curate for his father for ten years, only to find the gastronomic delights of rural Somerset a little wanting, and so he returned to Oxford, to New College, as a fellow and proctor in charge of discipline. It was unfortunate therefore when, after a particularly indulgent supper one evening, he was fined for having farted too loudly 'while pissing in the Senior Common Room'. In true Woodforde style, the fine extracted from our hero was a number of bottles of very fine port.

Eventually, in 1774, Woodforde left Oxford for good and became Vicar of Weston Longville, a tiny village in Norfolk. Here he settled down to a middle age devoted almost exclusively to the pursuit of good food and drink. He began to pay someone else to take most of the services (although he did deign to lead worship at Easter and Christmas and took a particular joy in christenings, perhaps due to the inevitable bunfight afterwards). He set up a small farm, a place for brewing his own beer and cider, and began to convene a supper club for nearby gastronomes. His diary is phenomenal both for the detail with which the parson describes his menus and the sheer size of them. For instance, in 1795 (when Britain was supposed to be tightening her belt in order to survive the blockade inflicted by revolutionary France), Woodforde sat down to a dinner of 'a couple of boiled chickens, a pig's face, a good pea soup, a fine rump of beef, a prestigious turkey and some macaroni' followed by 'batter custard pudding, jelly, apple fritters, tarts, raspberry puffs, baked apples, brandied cherries and various other sweets and desserts' all washed down with 'strong beer, porter, wine, port, sherry and strong malt liquor'. Although it was the fashion in Georgian

England to eat a small amount of lots of dishes, there can be no escaping that Woodforde had a sizeable appetite for both food and drink. Given that this menu was by no means atypical for him, it is a miracle that the parson was able to stand, let alone lead a service.

However, despite its author's unusually prodigious appetite, Woodforde's diary is considered of particular value to historians today precisely because of its ordinariness. It is filled with his little complaints, such as when he vents his irritation at having to go to Norwich to preach (a distance of, at most, eight miles) or criticises the King's Arms inn for its tiny plum puddings. But it also contains his little pleasures – the joy when he records how much he loved a particular supper, in 1797, of crab, veal, steak and trifle (among other things) is tangible. There are also glimpses into the genuine care he showed for his parishioners, for example his habit of inviting the poor and lonely to his house on Christmas Day for a veritable feast of puddings. Sometimes his methods were a little eccentric, such as his (admittedly successful) attempt to cure a serving boy of a cold by giving him a large glass of gin and then throwing him into a pond, but his feelings for his flock were genuine. Woodforde must have had the constitution of an ox as, even in his sixties, he was drinking and eating amounts that would floor most people today, but in 1803 his diet finally got the better of him. The good parson, however, is not without a legacy; not only is his diary now a must-read for historians and gourmands alike, but the pub where he was so crushingly short-changed on his plum pudding was later renamed the Parson Woodforde in his honour.

VI

The Reverend Jack Russell,
Vicar of Swimbridge (1795–1883)

The Sporting Parson

For many people, the Church's relationship with the world of flora and fauna is predicated on the sort of theology found in the hymn 'All Things Bright and Beautiful', with the ideal clergyman being a sort of heaven-sent park keeper, tending to the pastoral needs of 'all creatures great and small'. Such individuals are perhaps better off kept in the dark about the Reverend Jack Russell. Russell was considered by contemporaries to be the finest huntsman ever to have walked upon English soil and, when he wasn't hunting foxes or shooting birds, he spent his time engineering the breeding of vast numbers of horses and, most famously, dogs, in order to find the best specimens for his sporting needs. In his spare time, he also happened to be the Vicar of the Devon village of Swimbridge for nearly fifty years.

Russell grew up in the Devon countryside and, from an early age, his stated ambition was to be the finest horseman in England. His passion for field sports was evident during his time at school, where he kept a secret pack of dogs in some outbuildings, the discovery of which nearly resulted in his expulsion. Russell, however, survived the ire of his headmaster and, in 1814, he went to Exeter College, Oxford, where a chance encounter with the milkman was to ensure his place in history. Russell showed little aptitude for and even less interest in his academic studies; he was already, however, famed as an expert on horses and dogs. Russell was in the habit of waking early in order to get a full day in the saddle. One morning, as he arrived in the small village of Marston, a mile or so from Oxford where the hounds were kept, he happened to bump into the village milkman doing his rounds, followed by his little terrier who went by the name of Trump. The animal had distinctive tan markings on her face and tail, as well as an athletic physique; Russell was captivated and asked the milkman to name his price. Russell was convinced that she was the best specimen he had seen and, such was the prolificacy of his breeding programme, he developed his own signature breed, now, of course, called the Jack Russell Terrier.

Russell was ordained in 1819 and he and Trump moved back to the West Country where he acted as his father's Curate (although most of his time seems to have been spent amassing an even larger collection of dogs) until 1831, when he was appointed Vicar of Swimbridge. Russell soon became a well-known figure as he galloped across the Devon moorland, with his unique cry (attested to as sounding like he was shouting 'view-halloo') known for miles around. His riding skills were particularly admired by local gypsies, who respected him so much that they routinely left him trinkets in their wills, a rare bounty given that they were famous for their dislike of the clergy of the Established Church. His love of country pursuits was not, however, as popular with his Bishop. Henry Philpott, the notoriously irascible Bishop of Exeter, was furious that Russell seemed to spend a lot of time on horseback and very little time attending to the needs of his parishioners. Russell managed to prove that he had not in fact neglected his parish and, given that the hounds and horses were paid for from the considerable fortune of his wife (his exploits and gallantry had won the heart of an heiress in 1826), he responded to Philpott's probing by saying that he didn't see that they were any of the Bishop's business.

Russell's escape from his Bishop was fêted by his parish and high society alike. His fame as an equestrian spread far and wide, resulting in peers, playboys and even the Prince of Wales journeying down to Swimbridge to have the privilege of riding out with the Vicar. Russell's newfound fame did nothing to sap his energy: he continued his dog breeding, helping to found the Kennel Club in 1873, reintroduced a stag hunt to control the deer population on Exmoor and toured the county trying to encourage young men to take part in an annual wrestling competition against Cornwall. He ended up spending his wife's sizeable fortune sponsoring sports of all kinds, travelling far and wide to judge contests, and becoming something of a Victorian celebrity. All the while he kept his famously earthy Devonian charm, insisting on serving Devon cream and cider to all who visited the rectory, be they prince or peer, prodigious in his capacity for strong language while in the saddle and vociferous in his dislike of Cornwall.

Having frittered his wife's fortune on his escapades, Russell was forced, in 1880, to abandon his beloved Swimbridge and take up the more lucrative parish of Black Torrington, where his hunting friend Lord Poltimore ensured he was well looked after for the final three years of his life. 'The Sporting Parson' has not been forgotten in Swimbridge, where the pub is now named after him, inside of which a portrait of Russell's beloved Trump has pride of place. It is, however, only a copy. The original was commissioned by one of Jack Russell's great hunting friends, the man who would go on to become King Edward VII, and so now the little milkman's dog from Marston village has her place among the kings and queens of yore in the private collection at Sandringham.

VII

The Reverend Jeremiah Carter,
Curate of Lastingham (1701–c.1780)

Yorkshire's Pint-pulling Priest

There was a time when a clerical career was a job for life, a sinecure guaranteed to see the incumbent into old age in relative comfort and one that certainly did not require taking on odd jobs to make ends meet. These days, however, with clerical stipends a fraction of what they once were, it is not uncommon for certain clergy to juggle other jobs – lawyers, doctors, *Guardian* columnists, that sort of thing. While these illustrious professionals in Holy Orders may seem like a new phenomenon, they actually stand in a long tradition of clergy holding down multiple jobs. Perhaps the most notable of their antecedents was the Reverend Jeremiah Carter who, as Curate of a Yorkshire village for over twenty-five years, tended to his congregation's spiritual needs in more ways than one; he was both their Priest and the landlord of the village pub.

How Carter came to Lastingham is something of a mystery. He was a native of Chester and was made a Deacon there in 1725. By 1743, however, he had been appointed to be Curate on the edge of the North York Moors. Carter was of a class of clergyman very typical in the eighteenth century. He was probably of a poorer background, with perhaps only a limited education, and was employed by the Vicar to do the actual day-to-day work of the parish Priest. Carter's Vicar was the Reverend Luke Smelt, who not only held the title of Vicar of Lastingham for sixty years (and was paid the salary for it) but was also paid to be Vicar of a number of other parishes at the same time. However, Smelt did not visit Lastingham if he could avoid it, preferring to spend his time in York or London finding ways to prosecute Quakers, a quiet and unassuming sect for whom he had a surprisingly vicious dislike. From his combined salaries Smelt employed poorer clergy like Carter to do his work for him, paying the paltry sum of twenty pounds, which would be the equivalent of a salary of a little over £2,000 in today's money.

Carter was considered something of a charmer and had managed to win himself a beautiful, young wife. Married life was clearly congenial to the Carters, as they had produced no fewer than thirteen children by the time Jeremiah took the job in Lastingham. It soon became clear that the miserly salary paid by Smelt would not support such a sizeable family and so, when the tenancy of the village pub became available, the Carters became landlord and landlady. The charms of Mrs Carter kept the men of the village entertained while her clergyman husband led the villagers in dancing. Each Sunday, Carter finished his service, grabbed his violin and headed up something not dissimilar to a conga line of parishioners who danced and sang all the way to the pub, where Carter would change out of his preaching bands and start pulling pints. He was like the Pied Piper, where the rats were congregants and the river was ale.

The Carters' dual occupancy of pub and pulpit proved remarkably popular, with the fame of the dancing Curate of Lastingham and his buxom, beer-serving wife spreading across North Yorkshire. When, in 1764, Carter filed a report of over 250 people coming to receive Holy Communion (larger than the probable population of the tiny moors village at the time), the Church authorities became suspicious. Rumours of the Curate's sideline reached the Archdeacon (they had reached the Vicar, too, but he patently didn't care) and he contacted Carter demanding an explanation. Carter's reply shows that his time spent dealing with difficult characters in the pub was not wasted. The Curate wrote to his superior saying, 'My parishioners enjoy a triple advantage, being instructed, fed and amused all at the same time. Moreover, this method of spending their Sunday is so congenial with their inclinations, that they are imperceptibly led along the paths of piety and morality.' The wily clergyman also pointed out that his position at the bar and at the altar meant that he could keep an eye on anyone who was drinking too much, and that his fiddle playing and encouragement of dancing meant that his parishoners were too worn out to gossip or misbehave in other ways at the end of the evening. Carter's claim to be killing several birds with one stone silenced the Archdeacon, and for the next decade or so the dancing cleric and his beloved barmaid made sure that the needs of the people of Lastingham, be they funerals or fiddle music, baptisms or beers, were very well taken care of indeed.

VIII

The Very Reverend William Buckland, Dean of Westminster (1784–1856)

A 'Noah in Reverse' Who Gobbled up the Heart of the Sun King

The very nature of ordained ministry is such that it leaves room for hobbies. From the parson-naturalists who used their education to explore the world around them to twentieth-century Vicars obsessed with steam trains, it is almost expected that Priests take some time off from their good work to indulge in something that is of particular interest. Dean William Buckland had the most unusual and perhaps most ambitious of these hobbies, as, in a bizarre reversal of the task of Noah, it was his stated aim to eat one of every animal alive on earth.

Buckland had a particularly strange relationship with the natural world. On the one hand, he was considered the greatest naturalist of his time, providing us with the first complete excavation and categorisation of a dinosaur and discovering the Red Lady of Paviland, the oldest known ceremonial burial in Western Europe. On the other hand, he believed that the faeces of an animal were by far the most interesting of its features and had an insatiable desire to taste everything he came across, including, revoltingly, the aforementioned faecal matter.

Buckland attended Oxford, becoming the first person ever to study geology at the university and, after his degree, was ordained as a Priest in 1809. He then embarked on a career lecturing, often bringing a horse into the lecture theatre so he could sit upon it and instruct his students in the manner of a general. His eccentricities were manifold: he insisted on conducting all his work, including the muddy business of excavation, dressed in full academic garb of gown, hood and mortarboard, and would often teach while carrying a large hyena skull as a prop. On one occasion he hurled himself towards a student and, with the skull inches away from the hapless individual's face, demanded of him, 'What rules the world?' The petrified undergraduate stammered that he didn't know, at which point Buckland thrust the skull still closer and pronounced, 'The stomach, sir! The stomach rules the world. The great ones eat the less, and the less the lesser still.' The practical application of this maxim was to be his life's work.

In 1825 Buckland was made a Canon of Christ Church Cathedral in Oxford. In his canonry he and his wife Mary (also an accomplished zoologist who pioneered the use of the microscope to study marine zoophytes) would serve up infamous dinners designed to help fulfil William's ambition. Mice on toast was a popular breakfast treat *chez* Buckland, as was porpoise, of which the clergyman was particularly fond. Some animals, however, Buckland decided he only need eat once; mole fricassée and a snack of bluebottles were, it seems, too disgusting even for a man who ate droppings.

However, it wasn't only in the civilised milieu of a dinner party that Buckland sought to try new delicacies. He was always on the lookout for a chance to taste something novel. When on a visit to France, Buckland was being shown around a cathedral which claimed a miracle whereby the blood of a local saint was supposed to appear at certain times on the flagstones near the altar. Buckland, keen to uphold both Anglican rationality and try something esoteric, immediately got on his hands and knees and began licking the floor. After a short interval he got up again and proclaimed the miracle 'nonsense – I'd know the taste anywhere, this is very clearly bat urine'.

Perhaps Buckland's most infamous episode in his quest to push the boundaries of the edible occurred on another clerical visit. In 1845, he was appointed to the post of Dean of Westminster Abbey, and, by way of celebration, he and a small party of other dignitaries were invited to visit the then Archbishop of York's family home at Nuneham Courtenay to see the Prelate's collection of curiosities. Pride of place was given to the embalmed heart of French King Louis XIV, which had been smuggled to England after the French Revolution. The royal organ was passed round until it came to Buckland who exclaimed, 'I have eaten many strange things, but I have never eaten the heart of a king before', and promptly gobbled it up.

His love of science continued to the end of his life – in 1851 he had the second known example of Foucault's pendulum (a device that remains perpetually in motion due to the rotation of the earth) installed in the nave of Westminster Abbey. The menu at the Deanery later included puppy, panther and crocodile, and tours invariably took in his favourite piece of furniture – a desk made from fossilised dinosaur faeces. Buckland died in 1856 but he passed on his peculiar tastes to his son Frank who, when he heard that the starving inhabitants of Paris were forced to eat the animals in the city's zoo during the siege of 1871, immediately booked tickets to France in order to continue his father's bizarre culinary quest.

PRODIGAL SONS

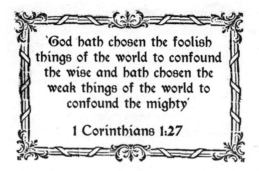

'God hath chosen the foolish things of the world to confound the wise and hath chosen the weak things of the world to confound the mighty'

1 Corinthians 1:27

Quite what is meant by 'success' in a clerical career is not particularly easy to pin down. Unlike their secular brethren, clergy are supposed to have an eye on the long game – by which is meant eternity. As such, determining which Priests are or are not 'successful' would require an unreasonably intimate knowledge of the beyond. While a clergyman might choose to count heads on a Sunday or even count the coins on the collection plate, it is pretty clear that mere numbers cannot be a measure for 'success' when one's primary battleground is not the spreadsheet but the soul.

The figures in this section are neither hardnosed bruisers who fought their way to prominence, but nor are they necessarily meek and mild. However, whether as a result of rising through the ranks of the Church as Bishops or Archbishops, becoming the most renowned wit of their day, accidentally being acclaimed as a sporting icon or, through quiet heroism, saving thousands of lives, each could be considered a 'success' in one way or another. They can all be considered

'Prodigal Sons'; figures who, like the son in the parable in St Luke's Gospel, ended up fêted against the odds. Very often their circumstances, early lives or personalities were less than auspicious and yet, in the end, they found themselves celebrated for one reason or another. In some cases their prodigal status manifested itself in terms of professional preferment or administrative efficiency despite manifest oddity or disinterest, but in others it has been necessary to defer to the old adage *vox populi, vox Dei*. Congregations are, after all, the people who see clergy week in week out; if they can't tell clerical saint from sinner, then no one can.

As befits biographies of those who all (ostensibly) believed in the Resurrection, no distinction is made between success in life and success post-mortem – while some climbed the dizzy heights of the ecclesiastical hierarchy, several of these clergy departed this life forgotten, only for their impact to become clear later. They were all individuals who, in any other career, would have been disastrous; indeed, in a secular context many would be considered unemployable. From their idleness to their inappropriate comments, their strange habits to their downright stubbornness, these are men who would, according to conventional wisdom, be considered weak and foolish in equal measure. And yet, for all their failings, they all made their mark on the world – some in ways that affected millions, others through just one life changed for the better.

Regrettably, the leading clergy of today no longer aspire to win the Polar Medal, blame social democracy for weak tea or shout 'BALDOCK' at random intervals.

They are engaged in chairing meetings, managing figures and studying for MBAs. Typically, just as the reputation of corporate jargon and practice reaches its lowest ebb in the secular world, the Church of England has sought to embrace it with open arms. As such, unlikely as these successes might have seemed in the past, they would be nigh on impossible now. Political changes in the last few decades mean that the Church now appoints its own senior figures without input from anyone else. As a consequence, the generations of lunatics, curmudgeons and visionaries inflicted on the Church in either strokes of bureaucratic genius or as the result of elaborate civil service jokes have, regrettably, come to an end.

There will always be eccentrics, rogues, bon viveurs and bizarre intellectuals among the clergy, but it is difficult to see a future for the brave and brilliant, but often irascible or insane individuals of the sort detailed in this section. They have been sacrificed to the idol of earnestness, to the cult of taking-things-seriously. The result of this is not that the Church has won back some great lost dignity but, by fearing the difficult or eccentric, has diminished her pool of talent and made herself seem less human, ironically rendering the institution even more ridiculous than before. It is always sensible to remember, dear reader, that God (like many of the characters described in the following pages) does appear to have a sense of humour after all.

I

The Most Reverend and Right Honourable Michael Ramsey, Archbishop of Canterbury and Primate of All England (1904–88)

'He is totally unsuitable to be Archbishop of Canterbury'

One evening during the spring of 1961, a short figure in a thick black overcoat, seemingly oblivious to the unseasonably warm weather, climbed up the steps of Admiralty Arch on the Mall. The man was Geoffrey Fisher, the weary outgoing Archbishop of Canterbury. Fisher had become Prelate during the dying days of the Second World War after the government's first choice to lead the Church of England into the brave new postwar world, William Temple, dropped dead after barely two years on the job. By the start of the swinging sixties, Fisher was increasingly worn down by life and cynical about the future; when asked his views on nuclear proliferation he replied laconically that 'the worst the bomb can do is sweep a large number of people from this world into the one they must eventually go to anyway'.

Fisher used to meet with the prime minister, Harold Macmillan, who was living temporarily in a cramped flat in Admiralty Arch while Downing Street was being refurbished. Macmillan dreaded his meetings with Fisher, complaining that 'whilst I always want to talk about religion the Archbishop will insist on talking politics'. Fisher announced his intention to resign as Archbishop and, unable to suppress the inner school teacher (he had run Repton School prior to being a Bishop), decided to offer Macmillan some advice on his successor. 'Whomever you choose,' Fisher began in his most authoritative tone, 'it must not be the Archbishop of York. He is a theologian, a scholar and a man of prayer. And he is totally unsuitable to be Archbishop of Canterbury. I would know – I was his headmaster.' Macmillan smiled and with the sort of imperturbability for which he was to become famous said, 'Thank you, your Grace, for your kind advice. However, whilst you may have been Dr Ramsey's headmaster, you were not mine.' He duly appointed Michael Ramsey as Archbishop.

To be fair to Fisher, Ramsey was not the obvious choice.

The child of a socialist and a suffragette, he had been a Congregationalist until his twenties and had a brother who, until his tragic early death, was Britain's most prominent atheist. On top of these unlikely origins, Ramsey was noted for having somewhat strange habits. As a child he used to spend hours careering round his parents' house trying to touch every wall in as quick succession as possible, and he used to enrage fellow students at theological college by spending chapel services tearing his handkerchiefs into strips. His tics could be verbal as well as physical. One young clergyman who had been enlisted to drive Ramsey from London back to Cambridge when he was a professor there in the 1950s recalled how, when they happened to pass through the Hertfordshire village of Baldock, Ramsey was so taken with the name of this unassuming market town that he spent the rest of the journey bellowing it out of the car window at the top of his voice.

At times he was just plain forgetful – such as when he locked a group of American airmen in Durham Cathedral as a Canon there during the war. Ramsey was supposed to be giving them a tour but got separated, forgot why he was there and decided to lock up as usual, leaving the men from Milwaukee to spend a chilly night huddled around the tomb of St Cuthbert. A number of behavioural experts have tried retrospectively to diagnose Ramsey, with conclusions varying from a mild form of attention deficit disorder to some form of autism. Regardless of the reasons behind Ramsey's behaviour, his manifest eccentricities meant that he was an unusual choice as the hundredth occupant of the throne of St Augustine.

While certain aspects of the job challenged him (visits to Sandringham were, for instance, dreaded by both the Royal Family and the Archbishop himself because of Ramsey's inability to keep still or make small talk), in other areas he proved himself more than equal to the task of leadership. The strength of his support for decriminalising homosexuality probably carried the bill through the House of Lords, and his rigorous opposition to apartheid in South Africa enabled the Anglican Church there to take a leading role in attempts to dismantle the system of white minority rule. He could also show flashes of wit – when asked by an eager cleric, looking for approval for an academic project, whether a comprehensive dictionary of heresies existed, he replied, 'Of course it exists, it's called *Hymns Ancient and Modern.*' Eventually, the constant battle to be understood and to lead the unwieldy Church became too much – it was said that by 1974 he would start each day by bashing his head on his desk three times and repeating the mantra 'I hate the Church of England' before he could bear to open his correspondence. Perhaps unsurprisingly, Ramsey resigned later that year.

Retirement, however, only caused the plot to thicken. Ramsey moved to Durham where, in 2009, some two decades after his death, a strange series of discoveries were made in the River Wear near the Archbishop's retirement home. A pair of amateur divers found a large number of gold and silver coins, medals and crucifixes near where the river flows past the cathedral close. Any hopes of an Anglo-Saxon hoard quickly dissipated when they were all found to be linked to key events Ramsey had attended – from a medallion commemorating his opening of a church in India to a crucifix thought to have been presented to the Archbishop by Pope Paul VI. The scattering of the items suggested that they had actually been thrown in over a period of some years. As always with Ramsey, this seeming eccentricity has a somewhat endearing reason behind it.

Ramsey found he had far too many possessions to fit into his Durham house as he downsized from Lambeth Palace. He had tried selling some items in aid of charity, but this had caused such offence to those who had originally given them to him that, in order to avoid further embarrassment, the perpetually shy Ramsey elected to chuck them into the icy waters of the Wear instead. As the reasons behind the bizarre watery fate of the objects became clear, an old friend is said to have chuckled knowingly and simply remarked: 'That is so Michael Ramsey'.

II

The Right Reverend Launcelot Fleming, Bishop of Norwich (1906–1990)

Helicopters and Heroism: The Unlikely Career of the 'Space Bishop'

Of all the clergy in this volume, Bishop Launcelot Fleming is arguably the most difficult to categorise; not because he is unexceptional but, rather, because he was a figure who displayed an abundance of distinguishing features. He was an impressive academic and a thoroughgoing eccentric; a brave adventurer and a famous bon viveur. Fleming, the son of a Scottish doctor, was indubitably bright. His childhood passion for geology led him to study the subject at both Cambridge and Yale, but, to the surprise of some contemporaries, he eschewed a career as a professional geologist and opted to take Holy Orders instead.

Fleming was ordained in 1934 and, rather than

becoming a Curate somewhere like most clergy (Fleming was, as we shall see, not one for convention), immediately became Chaplain of his old college, Trinity Hall, where he spent exactly one week in the post before taking a year out on sabbatical in order to accompany an expedition to the island of Spitsbergen in the Arctic Circle. During his absence Trinity Hall decided, as only a Cambridge college can, to promote Fleming to the crucial role of Dean (he would have been in Svalbard at the time). As with the post of Chaplain, the Dean's position was not a job that Fleming bothered spending too long getting to know about: it was a matter of months before Fleming had left Cambridge again in favour of Antarctica. Fleming was not, however, merely an amateur; his contribution to the British Antarctic Expedition was considered so significant that, on his return in 1937, he was awarded the Polar Medal by King George VI for his bravery and research.

The Second World War somewhat interrupted Fleming's Antarctic exploits. However, the fighting afforded him plenty of new avenues for adventure and, in 1940, he became a Royal Navy Chaplain. Fleming spent the war patrolling the Mediterranean and, despite being on board HMS *Queen Elizabeth* when she struck a mine, seems to have thoroughly enjoyed himself. He was of practical as well as spiritual use onboard – his small, wiry frame made him the perfect size for cleaning the ship's guns, which was achieved by wrapping the Chaplain in a large cloth then hauling him through the barrel. After 'a good war' Fleming was expecting to return to a long, quiet career studying glaciers in Cambridge (he was invited, in 1946, to become Director of the Scott Polar Institute). What he, and probably much of the Church of England, was not expecting was that he would be made a Bishop.

However, in 1949 that is exactly what happened. Fleming was initially reluctant, but Portsmouth had such close links to the navy that he found it impossible to resist. Despite having been ordained for fifteen years, his ministry had mostly been confined to Cambridge colleges, warships and the continent of Antarctica; Fleming was now in charge of 150 parishes, despite never having set foot in one. On his first day in the job he had to have the concept of a Parochial Church Council (your basic church committee) laboriously explained to him and it soon became clear that his intention was to delegate almost everything to his Archdeacons. Against the odds, Fleming's unorthodox approach appeared to have worked again with Portsmouth becoming so well run that, ten years after arriving there, the reluctant Bishop was on the move again, this time promoted to the diocese of Norwich.

Fleming's extreme delegation meant that he had a great deal of time for his other interests. He spent prolonged periods visiting the naval base while at Portsmouth. He enjoyed his long conversations with sailors and officers so much that he would routinely overrun and be late for other meetings. The affection was clearly mutual as, when Fleming realised the time, they often dropped him off in one of the naval helicopters. This particular favour earned the Bishop a stern ticking off from First Sea Lord Louis Mountbatten when Fleming used a naval helicopter to fly all the way to Lambeth Palace to avoid being late for a meeting with the Archbishop of Canterbury. Beyond the navy, Fleming found other japes to occupy his time: he sought out a suitable railway on which to fulfil his lifelong dream of riding on the footplate of a train, which he managed in 1960; he also became the only Bishop in modern times to single-handedly pilot a bill through parliament (a bill indicating British acceptance of the Antarctic Treaty of 1959, which is still in force today).

Fleming's unique approach to his duties meant he also found time to continue the flourishing social life that he had enjoyed in Cambridge. He was a member of numerous societies and dining clubs and was much in demand as a dinner companion. It was on his return from a well-lubricated meeting of one such dining club in 1962 that Fleming met the woman who would become his wife. Fleming had been out with the 'Nobody's Friends' club, a group of High Church clergy with famously large appetites for both food and wine. The little Bishop of Norwich had done his best to keep up but, by the time he arrived back at the London house of the friends with whom he was staying, he was a little worse for wear. Somewhere on his journey back, Fleming had picked up and put on a motorbike helmet. When one Jane Agutter came downstairs after hearing a mighty crash, she found the Bishop wandering down the hallway in his new headgear singing 'I'm a space Bishop' in a cod-liturgical voice. Quite why this made such an impression on Jane we'll never know but, three years later, when Fleming was fifty-eight, she agreed to marry him.

Fleming remained active into his advancing years. It was a particular tragedy for him, therefore, when he was struck down with a rare spinal disorder during his time at Norwich, making mobility difficult. He had always been popular with the Royal Family and so, in 1970, he resigned his see and moved to become Dean of Windsor. The gentler pace of life suited him, even if the bickering of the chapel's Canons did not. Eventually old age did what hypothermia and German mines could not and, in 1990, Fleming died peacefully at home with his medals and his wife (although not his motorcycle helmet) at his side.

III

Canon Sydney Smith,
Canon of St Paul's Cathedral (1771–1845)

'His jokes were sermons and his sermons jokes'

Sydney Smith was something of a legend in his own time. Renowned as 'the Smithiest of Smiths and the Wittiest of Wits', people travelled from all over the country – indeed, all over the world – to hear Smith hold forth on various subjects. From sharp one-liners to whole evenings taking centre stage as a raconteur, Smith was Regency England's top stand-up comedian. He was also, from 1796, a clergyman in the Church of England. The combination of this most serious of jobs with this least serious of men should not, according to received wisdom, have worked, but Smith was one of a kind.

Smith's talent for words was spotted early on. He was a schoolboy at Winchester College where, dismayed at the absolute dominance of Sydney and his brother at annual prize-giving, the other pupils signed a petition and refused to enter any more exams if the Smiths were also sitting them. He continued to excel at Oxford and, after being made a Deacon in 1796, went to Edinburgh to continue his studies. His relationship with Scotland was a mixed one – he described it as 'a land of Calvin, oatcakes, and sulphur' – but, as well as being where he met his wife, it was also the place he first found fame. While he was supposed to be studying, Smith became renowned as a preacher, as a dinner party guest and as the editor of the *Edinburgh Review*. Smith's motto with regard to book reviews was a prime example of his unique style: 'I never read a book before reviewing it; it prejudices a man so.' Alongside his reviews,

Smith published a series of articles supporting the Whig party's line on Catholic Emancipation and so, in 1806, he was rewarded by his new friends in high places with the post of Vicar of Foston and Thornton-le-Clay in Yorkshire.

The post in Yorkshire was intended to be a stepping stone to greater things. However, unfortunately for Smith, the Whigs lost a general election one year later, ushering in more than twenty years of Tory government. Smith was stuck in a place that was, in his own words, 'so far out of the way that I was actually twelve miles from the nearest lemon'. Smith made no secret of his feelings about life in the countryside, remarking, 'country life is very good; the best in fact – for cattle'. Although he spent quite some time grumbling, he was clearly a success as a parish Priest, becoming well loved by his congregation who grew quite attached to their famous parson. (That said, expectations were not high – he was the first clergyman to bother living in the parish for over 150 years.)

Smith managed to get to London with a degree of regularity, where he was invariably fêted wherever he went. He even won round the notoriously anti-clerical Lord Byron, who marvelled at Smith's fusion of his two vocations, observing that 'his jokes were sermons, and his sermons jokes'. Smith was in much demand at society parties; an invitation was, however, no guarantee of immunity from Smith's acid tongue, which could occasionally border on cruelty. When one hostess breezed into the room, Smith exclaimed that she looked 'as if she had just stepped out of the Ark'. When another arrived, expecting appreciation of her fashionable new rose turban, Smith whispered to his companion, 'now I know the *true* meaning of the word grotesque'. His closest friends didn't escape either: when asked about the religious beliefs of his companion, the corpulent Henry Luttrell,

Smith replied that 'his idea of Heaven is eating pâté de foie gras to the sound of trumpets'. Even when he was back in Yorkshire he had a habit of poking fun at the pretensions of society. Once, when he was in the company of a particularly grand society hostess, he heard her exclaim her disappointment at the lack of deer in the parkland round about. Smith invited her to his rectory, where he had procured a pack of donkeys, onto the heads of which he had tied some antlers. In honour of her visit he let them loose in his modest garden, causing untold chaos all round.

In 1828, Smith finally managed to secure a promotion and moved to a canonry in Bristol. Then, in 1831, when Earl Grey headed up the first Whig majority for decades (it was said that the new prime minister's first words on entering Downing Street were 'at last I can do something for Sydney Smith!'), Smith finally got to move to London as a canon of St Paul's. His new role seemed to heighten his comic powers. There, no one was safe from his jokes. He insisted on calling a pre-eminent society beauty, Miss Allcock, by his own Latin nickname of *Domina Omnia Penis*. He even caused a minor diplomatic incident by referring to the United States' Secretary of State as 'a steam engine in a pair of trousers'. When he wasn't being waspish, he spent his time preaching around London and writing copiously. He lampooned the Romantic poets of the time by composing a poem aping their style but, instead of writing about love, Smith wrote an ode to salad. It begins, 'To make this condiment, your poet begs/the pounded yellow of two hard-boiled eggs'.

Despite his natural gift for comedy, Smith could be profound, too. Before his death in 1845, he counselled the readers of one of his final publications that 'to love and be loved is the greatest happiness of existence'. Smith also once said, 'it is the greatest of all mistakes to do nothing because you can only do little' and, if his career his testament to anything, it is to the fact that a little laughter can go an awfully long way.

IV

The Reverend William Webb Ellis, Rector of St Clement Danes (1806–72)

The Rule-breaking Rector Who Became a Sporting Legend

There can be little denying that, as a clergyman, William Webb Ellis was something of a disappointment. Throughout his entire career in Holy Orders only one particularly fiery sermon, surfing a wave of jingoism at the start of the Crimean War, elicited any attention either inside or outside the Church. By the time he'd taken up the easy parish of Magdalen Laver in Essex in 1855, he was spending most of his time in France where, in 1872, he died. Indeed, Webb Ellis's career was so devastatingly unimpressive that it wasn't until the 1950s that anyone could work out where he'd actually been buried. Yet, despite his failure to make an impression as a Priest, Webb Ellis's name is perhaps the most recognisable in this whole volume due to his role as a 'King Arthur' figure in the great foundation myth of rugby.

Webb Ellis was the son of an army officer who, when William was barely five years old, was killed during the Peninsular War at the Battle of Albuera, leaving William, his brother and his mother destitute. William's mother made a decision to move to the Warwickshire town of Rugby where the famous public school had a policy of free education for any boy living within a ten-mile radius of the town's clock tower. As a result of this geographically arbitrated benevolence, William was afforded one of the best educations available at the time. However, as his later performance at Oxford demonstrated, Webb Ellis's real passion was sport.

To say that Rugby School in the early nineteenth century lacked discipline would be an understatement. At one point, pupils were partially roasted over a fire, as depicted in the novel *Tom Brown's Schooldays*. This is just one example of the internecine violence and chaos that constituted daily life at the nation's leading educational establishments. Discipline wasn't only lacking in the classrooms and boarding houses, but on the sports fields as well. Given that organised sport had largely been encouraged as an alternative to brawling with boys from the town, the spectre of violence haunted the games fields. The rules of the various games were mostly decided by the boys themselves, with enormous variations from school to school, indeed from game to game.

Despite this acknowledged flexibility, the young Webb Ellis had something of a reputation for, as one contemporary put it, 'taking unfair advantages'. Football, as played at Rugby at the time, did allow for an individual to catch a ball but that was a cue for his team to stop where they were and kick the ball backwards. The legend goes that Webb Ellis, with 'a fine disregard for the rules of football', picked up the ball in his hands and ran forward, placing it with a great flourish in the goal. And so the game of rugby was born.

At least, that is what the statue of Webb Ellis says. There were, however, doubts about Webb Ellis's role from the very beginning. When it was put to a contemporary from Webb Ellis's schooldays that he was the primogenitor of the sport he simply guffawed and said, 'I wouldn't quote him as an authority on anything whatsoever.' Others doubted the

Webb Ellis story due to the nature of the school and the rules of the sport of the time, with one old boy commenting that 'it [running with the ball] was not absolutely forbidden... though a jury of boys would probably decide it was justifiable homicide if he'd have been killed running it in'. Eventually the Rugbeian Society for former pupils decided to act and, in 1895, set up a committee to determine who was the game's true originating genius. Their results were pretty inconclusive, although they were particularly sceptical of Webb Ellis's role. In fairness to the one-time Rector of St Clement Danes, he had been dead for over twenty years, so was hardly available to defend himself.

The findings of the committee were, like those of so many committees the world over, quite irrelevant. The Webb Ellis myth was too good a story to dismiss out of hand and so the idle, jingoistic Vicar became the poster boy for a whole sport. Alongside the statue at his former school, Webb Ellis's grave was restored at the expense of rugby fans after its rediscovery in the 1950s and, in 1987, the year of the first Rugby World Cup, the decision was made to name the trophy awarded to the winners after the plucky, if slightly dubious, Rector from Rugby. There are still those who challenge the prominence given to Webb Ellis but most rugby fans are happy to go along with the myth. One rugby historian described Webb Ellis as being like Voltaire's conception of God: 'If he didn't exist, it would be necessary to invent him.' It is difficult to think of a better epitaph for the plucky clergyman with an aversion to the rules, who would go on to become, in spite of himself, an international sporting legend.

V

The Reverend Joseph Wolff,
Vicar of Isle Brewers (1795–1862)

'The Sublime Vagabond'

It is a great sadness that the Reverend Joseph Wolff was never going to receive any form of preferment in the Church. Had he at least managed to be made a Canon, the epithet 'loose' would have been perfect for him. Wolff was, frankly, a danger to himself and others. Having spent his youth falling out with every religious affiliation he encountered, he finally ended up in the Church of England, via various sects of interesting provenance. He spent his middle age careering around the Middle East and Asia, convinced that he could find the lost tribes of Israel. Astonishingly, he not only managed to find a group of herdsmen with recognisable messianic beliefs in the middle of a Yemeni desert, but he also managed to pacify a murderous tyrant in Persia whom British intelligence officers had been trying to deal with for years as part of 'the Great Game' in Central Asia. His dotage was spent confined to a rectory in rural Somerset where, presumably, it was hoped that he might be restrained from causing any more chaos at home or abroad.

Wolff was born in northern Bavaria where his father was a rabbi in a series of small towns. Despite his father's profession, Joseph's time in the Jewish faith was short – at the age of seven, while arguing with a Christian neighbour (arguments were to become Wolff's forte), he was finally urged by the exasperated old man to go and read the prophecy of Isaiah. The incident sparked an interest in the second coming that was to last all Wolff's life. His parents reluctantly allowed him to attend the Lutheran school in nearby Stuttgart but, by the age of eighteen, he'd fallen out with them as well and become a Roman Catholic.

This new religious identity didn't exactly last long either. Wolff was desperate to leave what he considered the tedium of southern Germany and so applied to be a Roman Catholic Priest. Barely three years after his conversion, he was unceremoniously booted out of one of the Papal colleges in Rome where he'd gone to study Middle Eastern ancient and modern languages in the hope of pursuing his interest in the lost tribes of Israel. The documents relating to Wolff's expulsion refer to his constant 'obnoxiousness', his daily arguments with his professors and regular statements about the falsity of Catholic doctrine. And so, after a brief period locked up in a Swiss monastery to teach him a lesson, Wolff emigrated to England and embraced Anglicanism.

Only three years later, in 1821, Wolff was on the move again. He had developed a theory that there was a lost tribe from the biblical twelve tribes of Israel somewhere in the Asiatic land mass. During his time abroad he was routinely forced out of places by angry mobs as he sought to convert people to his unique religious views which, though mostly Anglican, were spiced with the views of various apocalyptic sects that proliferated in the early nineteenth century. Unsurprisingly, whether it was among the Eastern Orthodox in Palestine, the Jews of Baghdad or the Sunnis of Egypt, the strange, squinting figure who routinely came and bothered them about their views on Armageddon was not exactly a hit.

In 1836, he went out on a self-appointed humanitarian mission to 'rescue' the Anglican missionary Samuel Gobat, who would later become the Bishop of Jerusalem, from his sickbed in Ethiopia. Despite Wolff nearly losing his life a number of times, his mission was a success. From Ethiopia, Wolff travelled to Yemen, where, to everyone's surprise except his own, he finally managed to track down his 'lost tribe'. It was a nomadic Arab tribe whose members identified themselves as 'Rechabites' after a group who were supposed to have assisted Israel in their wars with Canaan in the Old Testament. Quite what this group thought of having their peaceful desert existence disturbed by an over-excitable little Anglican missionary is not recorded. Wolff travelled home via America where, in 1837, he finally found a Bishop who was mad (or lazy) enough to ordain him. He returned to England in triumph.

But Wolff's escapades didn't stop there. In 1843, emboldened by his remarkable ability to remain unmurdered in the most dangerous parts of the world, he again set out on one of his self-appointed rescue missions. Two British secret agents, Lieutenant Colonel Stoddart and Captain Connolly, were reported missing in the Central Asian emirate of Bukhara (now a city in Uzbekistan). They had been sent there to try and convince the bloodthirsty but powerful Emir of two things: firstly, to stop the wholesale murder of his non-Muslim subjects; and, secondly, to back British, rather than Russian, interests in 'the Great Game' as the two powers fought for control of Central Asia. What Wolff didn't know was that the Emir had already taken great pleasure in the public beheading of both men some time before he had even set out to rescue them.

The Emir, sitting behind the walls of the mighty Ark fortress, was informed that an ambassador from England had arrived. Already relishing the thought of another public beheading, he indicated that the emissary should be allowed in. The enormous doors of the fortress opened and in shuffled the preposterous figure of the Reverend Joseph Wolff who, convinced that no foreign potentate could possibly fail to be swayed by evidence of a Cambridge University degree, had dressed himself up in his full choir dress of cassock, surplice, preaching bands and, as the *pièce de résistance*, his academic hood indicating his MA from Cambridge. The Emir emitted a strange sound, and then proceeded to laugh uncontrollably for several minutes. Considering Wolff too ridiculous a figure to waste time beheading, the Emir sent the dumpy, overdressed cleric off back to London.

Although the Bukhara incident was the end of his 'rescue missions', Wolff continued to peddle his mad theories, never failing to bend a fact or turn a conversation onto his favourite topic of 'the lost tribes'. Clearly terrified at what he might do should he be allowed to leave the country again, various figures clubbed together and managed to find him the Vicar's job in Isle Brewers in Somerset on his return in 1845. There he remained, writing up his bizarre adventures, including the tale of how he had successfully cheated death where the cream of the British intelligence service had failed. His books proved hugely popular and were even translated into German. It is ironic that, in the corners of rural Bavaria, which he spent a whole lifetime running away from, people can now read about the strange life of the man they called 'the Sublime Vagabond'.

VI

The Right Reverend Douglas Feaver, Bishop of Peterborough (1914–97)

'The rudest man in the Church of England'

If one were to compile a list of attributes for the ideal Bishop, it is unlikely that brusqueness would be high on the list.

That is not to say that there is no scriptural support for a certain sharpness of tongue – from St Paul's barbed letter to the 'foolish' Galatians to Christ himself calling Peter 'Satan', Christianity has had plenty of precedent for priestly put-downs. Douglas Feaver, however, took this to a new level. Whether it was members of the General Synod ('they have seething bosoms, but nothing above'), his parishes ('there are only two types – the important and the self-important') or children ('all they do is leak at both ends!'), nobody was safe from Feaver's scorn. Yet, as a Bishop he was considered an enormous success; renowned for his timely and erudite contributions in parliament, respected as a community leader and beloved by the people of his diocese, who learned to take his remarks with a pinch of salt.

Born in 1914, Douglas Feaver was an academic prodigy. He won a scholarship to Keble College, Oxford, where he proceeded to gain double first-class degrees in both history and theology. Feaver's tongue soon proved as sharp as his mind, as the tutors who encouraged him to pursue academia soon found out. Instead, in 1938, he became a Curate at the Abbey in St Albans. His curacy was rapidly cut short by the advent of the Second World War. Being in excellent physical shape (he retained his imposing stature well into old age) and still only twenty-five, Feaver felt bound to enlist. He ended up joining the RAF, serving with some distinction in Egypt. Cruelly, for a man named Feaver, he became grievously ill with the eponymous affliction and it was said that he was kept awake by the sound of his own grave being dug outside the tent. Such experiences undeniably strengthened the will of the already forthright Feaver. It is also easy to see why, given the peril he had found himself in during the war, he found it so difficult in later years to treat some of the more ludicrous aspects of ecclesiastical life with the gravity they so often assumed.

After demobilisation, Feaver returned to St Albans and found himself rapidly promoted to canon. He was then called to bring his sense of disciplined liturgy, careful mind and caustic sense of humour to the main parish church in Nottingham, St Mary's. Though enormously popular in the parish and the city, he frustrated his superiors immensely. Feaver's great foe was his Bishop, Russell Barry, a man whose opinions on religion, politics and social niceties were about as far from Feaver's as was possible. On one occasion, as Feaver stood up to speak at a diocesan event, the Bishop made a great show of turning off his antiquated hearing aid before turning to his neighbour and instructing him to tell him when Feaver had finished. Given such enmity from the episcopal bench, it was something of a surprise when Feaver was nominated as Bishop of Peterborough in 1972.

It was as a Bishop that Feaver was allowed free rein to do and say exactly as he liked, and it was an opportunity of which he availed himself frequently. He made no secret of his lack of further ambition, stating at his very first diocesan synod that 'the undertakers can be my next removers and the Church Commissioners can pay'. This bristling contempt for the clunking mechanisms of the Church extended to his fellow Bishops: of one ultra-liberal colleague he famously said, 'he'll believe anything, providing it's not in the Bible'.

At official functions he could be dynamite. When Peterborough's new MP tried to introduce himself to Feaver on the logic that they were both, in his own, modest words, 'locally influential Christians', the Bishop took one look at his clammy outstretched hand and said, 'I'm afraid I don't shake hands with members of the Lower House'. However, his fellow members of the House of Lords were also subject to the Bishop's invective; he dismissed one peer by saying 'his mouth is for export and his head has no entrance'.

Invariably these important figures (although with Feaver's distinction between parishes in mind, we might more accurately call them self-important) took great umbrage at Feaver's manner – the Dean of Westminster even bestowed on him the epithet 'the rudest man in the Church of England'. However, the people who were most often at the receiving end, namely congregations, seemed to love the Bishop's cutting way with words. Confirmations afforded him ample opportunity to spread his insults across several counties. At one service, he asked some of the young men present if they knew the sort of girl they'd like to marry only to remark, while gesturing at the elderly members of the congregation with his Bishop's crosier, 'Mind you, there's not much of a choice here tonight.' At another confirmation, he was congratulating a woman after the service when she introduced him to her husband, only for a visibly shocked Feaver to ask, 'Where on earth did you find him – in a blackout?' Even something as simple as a cup of tea could provoke a tongue-lashing from the Bishop. During the 1980s, when the predecessors of the Liberal Democrats were the focus of much news coverage, Feaver recoiled from a particularly weak offering of tea at a parish event with the words, 'That looks like it was invented by the SDP.'

When, after over twelve years as Bishop, a reluctant and exhausted Feaver finally retired, his parishioners presented him with a copy of the collection of his witticisms and insults, which they had called 'Purple Feaver'. Feaver was genuinely touched, thanking them for their kindness in preparing 'this flight of fancy'. By stark contrast, when the press asked for a statement, they received a bluff 'no comment' instead. Thirteen years later, in 1997, the great poker of pretensions died aged eighty-three, a loss which may have returned colour to the faces of leaders in both Church and state, but undoubtedly took some away from the lives of those who had truly known him.

VII

The Reverend Charles Lowder,
Vicar of St Peter's, London Docks (1820–80)

Riots, Ritualism and Rotten Eggs

Charles Lowder was an undeniably difficult man. Described by contemporaries as 'imperious' and 'pernickety', he relished controversies (whiling away many an hour answering charges before magistrates) and spent his entire career ignoring the advice of his friends, colleagues and superiors and doing, essentially, whatever he damn well pleased. He also has the rare honour of having a day allocated to him in the Church of England's liturgical calendar, where it commemorates the great and the good of the Church's past (the closest Anglicans get to making new saints), and his legacy is still to this day propagated by the society he founded to carry on his principles.

After an ordinary childhood and university career, Lowder took Holy Orders and ended up as a Curate in rural Gloucestershire. However, at some point in 1850 he felt a great calling to the ministry in London and so, one year later, took up a position as an assistant Priest at St Barnabas, Pimlico. In the very year Lowder arrived, a journalist called Henry Mayhew published *London Labour and the London Poor*, a work that shocked Victorian society by painting a picture of a dirty, stinking megalopolis, teeming with beggars, prostitutes and mudlarks which told real tales of deprivation that made the works of Dickens look like a fairy tale. It was this world that Lowder felt a particular vocation to minister to. He married this strong call to serve the poor with a commitment to elaborate Anglo-Catholic worship, advocating the regular celebration of communion with as much ritual as possible. Candles, vestments, smells and bells – Lowder wanted it all. Both of these tendencies made him an instant outsider, mistrusted by both his Bishop and members of the laity.

It was during his time at St Barnabas that Lowder had his first brush with the law. While elections for Churchwardens are, nowadays, mind-numbingly soporific, in the nineteenth century they were often hotly contested. Lowder's rampant ritualism had provoked the ire of a number of local figures who felt the need to stand up against the innovations which they considered far too close to the ghastliness of continental popery. The leader of this group was a Mr Westerton, who, as part of his campaign strategy, employed a man to stand outside St Barnabas with a sandwich board, emblazoned with slogans attacking Lowder. Lowder, in a typically intemperate moment, paid some boys from the church's choir to source some rotten eggs and pelt the unfortunate canvasser. The boys duly did so, leaving the enraged man and his sandwich board in a mess of stinking yolks. Lowder's involvement in the pelting soon became known and, using the excuse of 'a moment of madness' (one of the first known examples of this catch-all apology for those caught red-handed), he was called in front of a magistrate and earned a suspension from his clerical duties.

On his return to ministry, Lowder decided to found a society for Priests committed to both ministry among the poor and Anglo-Catholic worship. On 28 February 1855, he became the first master of the Society of the Holy Cross, which still exists for the purposes set out by Lowder to this day. The society was known by the acronym SSC, which is from the Latin title of the group, *Societas Sanctae Crucis*. Some individuals, however, playing on popular prejudices about Catholicism as well as Lowder's own conspicuously unmarried status, suggested that it in fact stood for 'The Society for Sodomite Clergy'. In 1856 Lowder was on the move again, this time to the church of St George in the East, between Shadwell and Wapping, to head up a new mission chapel right in the midst of the East End. This church had long suffered attention from anti-ritualist mobs (who were angry that excessive ritual in church was part of a Roman Catholic conspiracy) and this corner of the East End, with its minimal adherence to law and order at the best of times, was now a powder keg of tension.

There was near constant trouble at the mission chapel Lowder had constructed at Wapping. Services were about as high in style as was possible, which provoked the ire of large crowds fearful of 'popish influences', but also probably looking to find a way to while away the time in the long, fetid months of the East End summer. Bricks would fly through the windows during Mass and drunken rioters would break in and sing bawdy songs over the hymns. Lowder refused to be intimidated – at one point he slammed a door on the face of an intruder with such force that he had to appear before a magistrate again. These public nuisances continued even when Lowder managed in 1866 to build his new church (St Peter's, London Docks) and showed no sign of stopping until, that summer, the East End was struck by a major outbreak of cholera.

It was here that Lowder, for all his pig-headedness, really earned his spurs. As doctors, policemen and, indeed, anyone else who could afford to, abandoned Wapping, Shadwell and Whitechapel, Lowder stayed put. He raised enormous amounts of money for medical supplies and shipped in volunteers to care for the dying. He showed no fear of the disease, spending hours traipsing round the parish delivering supplies and tending to the sick. Overnight, he became the hero of the East End. One image that lives on in East End folk memory is of Lowder in his cloak and cassock, carrying the body of a dead orphan through the filthy streets of Wapping so that he might give her a decent burial. It was this incident that earned him the title 'Father', the first Priest in the Church of England ever to be so called.

After the cholera abated, Lowder was seen in a new light. Children would follow him round the parish playing in the folds of his great flowing cloak; adults who had previously pelted him with stones now greeted him with reverence in the street, and attendance at his services sky-rocketed, with more than eight hundred people taking communion each Sunday morning. Lowder, in typical style, was not complacent and carried on working phenomenally hard.

In 1880, he was finally persuaded to take a holiday to Austria. However, the damage to his health from overwork had been done and it was there that Lowder died. When his body was returned to St Peter's for his funeral, crowds thronged the streets. Twenty years before, the police had been brought in to stop an angry mob from throwing Lowder in the docks. Now they were called to hold the line of weeping East Enders at bay, as they paid their final respects to the man they had come to call 'Father'.

VIII

The Right Reverend Howell Witt,
Bishop of North West Australia (1920–98)

'The Dowager Duchess of Dingo Creek'

Much has been written by theologians about the dignity of a Bishop's office, conjuring up images of earnest episcopal figures, much vexed by their own solemnity. Not so Howell Witt, who, whether he was being held captive by a group of belligerent schoolchildren, haplessly chasing sheep across the outback or touring his solo drag act around somewhat perplexed congregations, was the antithesis of solemnity.

Born to a dockworker and his wife in South Wales, Howell Witt bumbled through life with an irrepressible cheerfulness until one day, via a series of bizarre incidents, he ended up as a Bishop on the other side of the world. After training for the Priesthood among the monastic community at Mirfield in Yorkshire (a college which is, perhaps, more inclined than others to wink at early onset eccentricity), Witt went as Curate to the tiny Welsh town of Usk. The Vicar noticed Witt's genial and laid-back demeanour and suggested that he might wish to coordinate some summer holiday activities for the children of the parish. One day, as Witt was supervising a group of children playing in the vicarage, his charges started to tie him to his chair with some old rope that they had discovered. Witt, assuming it was all part of a game, merrily consented until he realised that he was bound fast. He could only watch in horror as the children he was supposed to be responsible for trotted merrily out of the door, leaving the luckless Curate thrashing around for several hours until he finally managed to free himself and round up his mischievous young parishioners.

After his curacy in 1948, Witt moved to Camberwell, south London, where he combined his role as a parish Priest, with playing rugby for London Welsh. His time in the capital was short-lived, however, as he was tempted out by the vague promise of a 'special job' from the Bishop of Willochra in South Australia. Only on his arrival did he learn that the 'special job' the Bishop had in mind was ministering to the Woomera Prohibited Area – nearly 50,000 square miles of bush in which the Australian military tested long-range missiles. Witt was less than happy at the double-cross, not least because it soon transpired he would also have to join the army, undergoing several weeks' gruelling training in the outback. It wasn't long before Witt got his revenge. A year or so into Witt's Chaplaincy, the Bishop, in the course of visiting some of his parishes, accidently strayed into the prohibited area and was picked up by an army patrol on the charge of trespassing. After protesting to the arresting officer in the strongest possible terms that he was the Bishop of Willochra, he was brought to Witt, as the area Chaplain, to be identified. Witt looked him up and down and then solemnly informed the officer that he had never laid eyes on the man in his life, leading to a prolonged confinement for the Bishop until someone more sympathetic could be contacted.

Woomera wasn't a totally barren placement for Witt, as it was at the church fête held on the base that he first premiered his drag act alter ego, 'The Dowager Duchess of Dingo Creek'. Witt arrived to open the fête plastered in make-up, dressed in a hooped skirt and with an enormous pretend bosom. Unfortunately, in a further twist that could only have happened to Witt, as he began proceedings two camels that were supposed to be part of a parade escaped their pen and began rampaging round the site. Witt hoisted up his skirt and gave chase. There are those still alive today who recall the image of the Anglican clergyman, running after the camels across the missile testing ground, a pair of fake breasts bouncing against his face and a tiara on his head.

After nearly a decade in Woomera, Witt moved to be a Priest of Elizabeth, just north of Adelaide. Here, his primary success was to convince the authorities that the discos he was holding to finance the construction of a new church building did, in fact, count as religious services and therefore were immune from noise complaints. In 1965, to his enormous surprise, he was elected Bishop of the largest land-based diocese on earth, that of North West Australia. The task of covering the pastoral needs of 150,000 people spread across over two million square kilometres would have daunted most people, but Witt relished it. Plane travel was a necessity and he soon honed the art of changing into his episcopal garb in the confines of an aircraft lavatory cubicle. The life of the vast outback diocese was hugely varied. Witt was taught the intricacies of Aboriginal goat hunting and also learned how to dip sheep, though they more often than not managed to get the better of him, resulting in the Bishop, once again, scampering across the outback in inappropriate clothing after recalcitrant livestock.

Witt loved the rough and tumble of North West Australia so much that he was palpably disappointed when he was promoted to the diocese of Bathurst, although he did express great joy at finally having a house with more than one loo. The 'Bush Bishop', as he was known, was bumbling, inappropriate and adventurous to the end. When he died in 1998, it transpired that he was midway through writing a church-themed erotic novel. His son, commenting after Witt's funeral, observed that, though the world had tolerated

'The Dowager Duchess of Dingo Creek', 'it probably wasn't ready for a Mills and Boon cassock ripper just yet'.

IX

The Reverend Donald Pateman, Vicar of St Mark's, Dalston (1915–98)

'The most politically incorrect clergyman in England'

For forty-two years, the Reverend Don Pateman ran the enormous nineteenth-century Gothic barn that is St Mark's, Dalston, with the motto 'Victorian architecture; Victorian outlook'. Whether writing lengthy pieces in support of corporal punishment in the parish magazine, instituting a work-to-rule policy for weddings insisting on dressing his choir in three-piece Eton suits, Pateman self-consciously cultivated the image of a man from a different era. And yet, in his commitment to youth work in a thoroughly deprived area of London, and in his innovation of Chaplaincy directed specifically towards the West Indian population, he was manifestly ahead of his time. Pateman was a complex figure whose eccentricity and old-fashioned views masked a thoroughly successful parish Priest.

Born in 1915, Pateman came to Holy Orders after serving in the RAF during the Second World War. He spent his entire ministry in the East End, serving curacies at Bethnal Green and in the bombed-out ruins of All Hallows, Bromley by Bow. Then, in 1956, he was appointed to be Vicar of St Mark's in Dalston, where he was to stay in the post until the year of his death. Pateman had very particular opinions about how churches should be run. He exclusively used the 1611 King James Bible and the 1662 Book of Common Prayer, and was adamant that his congregation should dress properly when attending worship. He eventually became so fed up with the standard of dress that he persuaded a local businessman to pay for an entire set of three-piece suits with wing collars for the choirboys. As one chorister recalled, dressing like Etonians in the heart of the East End not only pleased Pateman, but also had the side effect of forcing the choirboys to become very good at street fighting.

Despite his ministry being in one of the most advanced industrial cities on earth, Pateman affected a loathing for modernity in all its forms. He used to illustrate his parish magazine, not with pictures of his own parish, but with Victorian paintings of country cottages. Under one such chocolate box image he wrote: 'Study this charming picture carefully. No television aerial (thank God!), still less one of those hideous "dishes" (thrice may His name be praised!).' This unique mixture of religious enthusiasm and reactionary thought was not only limited to his commentary on aesthetics. Pateman made international headlines when he used his magazine to attack the home secretary's 1965 decision to abandon corporal punishment in schools. In an article, he referred to Roy Jenkins as 'a purring old pussy' and announced his intention to run a referendum of his own in the parish to demonstrate the rectitude of the birch. He duly did so and found his opinion backed up by nearly five thousand votes, prompting another article directed at the home secretary in which he helpfully suggested that flogging might provide an effective punishment for crimes as diverse as mugging and football hooliganism.

Alongside modernity, poor manners were another pet hate. He particularly loathed lateness and became so fed up with brides arriving late to their weddings that he introduced a sliding scale of fines which he would hand to couples at wedding rehearsals. Ten minutes meant they lost one hymn, twenty minutes meant two hymns and the wedding photographer was gone, twenty-five minutes meant the loss of all their hymns as well as the choir and organist, while half an hour meant that the wedding was cancelled altogether. Pateman's unique pastoral style was demonstrated again during the postal strike of 1971, when he announced that any postal workers seeking to get married in Dalston would have to have a 'work-to-rule' wedding. That meant no choir, no bells, no confetti, no photographs, no heating and no lighting. Pateman was, as ever, forthright in his reasoning: 'Postmen earn the same money as me. I went to university for three years and if I can be expected to live on twenty-one pounds a week, so should they!'

For all his bluff denunciations of modernity, Pateman was a remarkably successful clergyman. His scheme to welcome West Indian migrants (he even dedicated one of his curates to it full time) during a period when racism was endemic in British society was nothing short of visionary. It paid dividends, too, with the once small congregation of St Mark's swelled to several hundred by migrants loyal to the Vicar. Pateman was adept at getting what he wanted and, whether he was securing funding for clothing or cameras, he made sure that the community which he loved was well equipped. (He established one of the first youth photography clubs in the East End at the church, an opportunity which helped at least one child, Dennis Morris, who would go on to capture iconic shots of the Sex Pistols and Bob Marley and become a noted professional photographer in adulthood). When Pateman died, just months after grudgingly taking retirement, the irony was not lost on many that over a thousand people of all races, creeds and backgrounds turned out to mourn the man who had been referred to by one newspaper as 'the most politically incorrect clergyman in England'.

X

The Reverend Hugh Grimes, Chaplain of Vienna (1875–1962)

Schindler in a Surplice

Charles Hugh Duffy Grimes was a typical – one might even say ordinary – clergyman of his generation. He had been a scholar of Jesus College, Cambridge, where his primary interest had been in English regional history. In an age where clergy were not necessarily expected to hold theological matters as their primary interest, this proved no bar to Grimes and he ended up being ordained a Priest in St Albans in 1904. Initially, Grimes devoted much of his time to his passion for history, becoming particularly interested in the rather cheery subject of the history of divorce. In 1907 he took a job teaching in Australia, where he was to remain, undistinguished, for twelve years. During a parish job back in England, he mostly seemed to work on his new hobby, the study of migration. It was for his initially amateur research on this particular area for the Church Army that he was made a fellow of the Royal Geographical Society in 1924.

By now Grimes, at nearly fifty years old, had grown tired of even cursory forays into English parish life. With this admirably short curriculum vitae, he took the equivalent of early retirement and became Chaplain to a number of British expatriate communities scattered around Europe. From Barcelona to the fashionable resorts of Le Havre and Biarritz, Grimes spent the next decade laying his hat across the continent. By 1934, he had arrived in Vienna. Christ Church, the Anglican outpost in the city, was not a particularly grand affair – attached to the embassy due to an old Imperial law prohibiting non-Roman Catholic worship outside of areas with diplomatic privileges, the tiny chapel could accommodate 150 people at a push. Grimes remained there longer than in his other posts, until, in 1938, the storm clouds that had been building across Europe finally broke over Charles Hugh Duffy Grimes' quiet sinecure.

On 12 March 1938, German forces rolled over the border into Austria, bringing into effect the *Anschluss*. Suddenly, Grimes and his congregation were living under a Nazi regime. Over the four years he'd been serving in Vienna, Grimes had got to know and befriend members of the Jewish community. Recognising their panic and wary of the impending travel ban on Jews from Austria, the gentile Cambridge clergyman began to offer baptism to those who came to him, providing them with a safe ticket out of Nazi-occupied Vienna in the form of a baptismal certificate. Spring became summer and the persecution of Jewish homes and businesses increased; what had been a trickle of a few Jews with links to England became a flood. Grimes began holding several services a day: on 10 July he baptised and issued certificates for 103 people; on 25 July he baptised another 229, so the Anglican Chaplaincy became a revolving door for Jews desperate to find a loophole in tightening travel restrictions.

Grimes, aware of the heightened peril his Jewish

neighbours were in, teamed up with the naval attaché at the embassy, Captain Thomas Kendrick, and so Christ Church became the hub for counter-intelligence in the Austrian capital. Grimes even went so far as to appoint the British secret agent Fred Richter as the church's verger to provide cover for his activities. It was this link that spelled the end for Grimes. He was hastily recalled to London and accused of going beyond his remit, but not before he managed to secure a retired Anglican clergyman, Reverend Fred Collard, to take his place. Collard continued the baptisms and, by August that year, 1,800 Jews had been issued with certificates. Eventually the Gestapo cottoned on and raided the Chaplaincy during a baptism. They interrogated the sixty-eight-year-old Collard for three days. Badly beaten and unable to do any more, Collard followed Grimes back to England. Richter was not so lucky; he was eventually caught and sent to Auschwitz, where he died.

On his return, Grimes kept his pre-war adventures to himself, becoming Vicar of Newton Ferrers in Devon where he was largely remembered for skinny dipping on the beach near the town. He returned to an unfussy pattern of life, writing a dense local history and attending to his clerical duties until his death in 1962. Grimes' heroism only became known nearly forty years after his death. After research into the wartime Chaplain using archives only recently made accessible, the full extent of his activities became clear, leading Christ Church in Vienna to commission a plaque in 2013, featuring an image of the hastily scribbled registers in Grimes' hand. Today there are still a number of survivors of Nazi persecution who owe their lives to him.

ROGUES

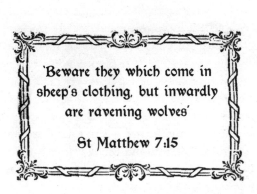

'Beware they which come in
sheep's clothing, but inwardly
are ravening wolves'

St Matthew 7:15

The Victorian era was one in which, if people could get things wrong, they generally did. Whether it was their preparations for the Second Boer War or their firmly held belief that the common cold could be cured by the application of Bovril, the denizens of the nineteenth century were masters of misconception. Perhaps the most egregious of their errors was the belief, regrettably passed on to consecutive generations, that Christianity is about being 'meek and mild'.

Even a cursory glance at the Victorian hymn gives a view of the Christian faith so sickly sweet that one runs the risk of developing diabetes. Much contemporaneous theology has, in other guises, sought to perpetuate the view that Christians are called to be grinningly optimistic about life, as well as obsequiously friendly to all and sundry. The concept that one of the most complex and influential thought systems in the history of humanity can be boiled down to 'being nice' was not only a monumental oversimplification but it also, more regrettably, almost put an end to the tradition of cutting Priests out of mad, bad and dangerous cloth. Vicars, as the public face of Christianity, had to be the epitome of the mild stereotype – gentle, inoffensive, and, ideally, boring to boot.

Those in the eighteenth century, as the figures in this section will show, held no such preconceptions. From piratical Archbishops to trespassing parsons, the Georgian Church was replete with big characters for whom a calling to Priesthood meant a subsidy for various adventures. If someone had told them that 'Jesus wants you for a sunbeam', they might have found themselves on the receiving end of physical violence. Indeed, theirs was a ministry totally compatible with a life of crime.

Some of the figures in the following section were emphatically bad, the 'wolves in sheep's clothing' warned of by the Bible. Others ended up living lives of roguery and adventure not because of any great rejection of the precepts of faith but, rather, because they were foolish or vain, or, in a couple of cases, simply had a low boredom threshold. These rogues serve as a reminder of a fact that is often forgotten, not least by Priests themselves, namely that the clergy are people, too. Despite the need to step out each Sunday and play the saint, they are prone to the lust, laziness and downright ludicrousness that constitutes the human condition. They are just as likely to inflate their own importance, have their hearts broken, or collect an enormous stash of French pornography (i.e. the Reverend Dr Edward Drax Free) as any other person. While they are called to 'have their conversation in heaven' they are squarely rooted on earth during their ministry.

This inherent tension can sometimes be creative – many are the saints or campaigners who have turned their inner turmoil into definitive action. Yet it can also be disastrous.

This section is not made up of the well-trodden exemplars of St Mary Magdalene, Thomas Becket or Martin Luther King but instead tells of chancers, wrong 'uns and adrenaline junkies who also happened to be called to serve as Priests. So, cast your tea cosy aside and meet some of the raunchiest, raciest, and most reckless vicars in the Church's history...

I

The Reverend James Hackman, Vicar of Wiveton (1752–79)

Madness, Murder and a Sandwich

As part of the liturgy for Holy Communion in the Book of Common Prayer, Church of England clergy are required to recite the Ten Commandments. They're not easy reading and remind the congregation that nobody's perfect and that we all almost certainly break one or two at some point or another. James Hackman, an infamous eighteenth-century clergyman, took this a little further, managing to break three in a single day.

Hackman was an attractive young man who had initially set out on an army career. However, while serving as an ensign in the 68th Regiment of Foot, he had the misfortune to meet and fall passionately in love with a glamorous society beauty, the singer Martha Ray. So far, so Jane Austen. Martha Ray reciprocated the young soldier's affection and the two began an affair. However, there was a slight complication – Ray was also the mistress of the enormously powerful Earl of Sandwich (of convenient-lunch-devising fame), the First Lord of the Admiralty. In fact, she had been something more than a mistress, living with Sandwich after his wife was declared insane and giving birth to five of his children. As such, the young officer could hardly compete with a peer of the realm and Ray, having appraised on which side her sandwich was buttered, broke off the attachment to Hackman.

James Hackman, however, was not a man who took no for an answer. Convincing himself that with better social standing and an increased income he might be able to win Ray back, Hackman left the army and undertook to be ordained in the Church of England (a decision that might seem questionable to anyone who has ever lived on a clerical stipend). By 1779 Hackman had been made a Priest and was awarded the rectory of Wiveton in Norfolk, but he never even so much as visited his church, preferring instead to stay in London, attending every society ball and party he could in a desperate attempt to resume his affair with Ray. Tracking her every movement, he began to suspect her of having taken a new lover. On 7 April 1779, barely a month after his ordination, he learned that she was to attend the theatre in Covent Garden and followed her there in a last-ditch attempt to win her hand. Unfortunately for Martha Ray, he observed her making small talk with Lord Coleraine, a member of parliament with a less than immaculate reputation. Hackman immediately concluded the worst, flew into a rage and went to fetch a brace of pistols.

A fruitseller at Covent Garden Market described what happened after the performance finished. 'The gentleman in black came up, laid hold of her by the gown, and pulled out of his pocket two pistols; he shot the right-hand pistol at her, and the other at himself.' Unfortunately for the Reverend James Hackman, he survived. Unfortunately for Martha Ray, she did not. Hackman had placed his pistol on Ray's forehead and blown her brains out; in the ensuing struggle he tried to do the same to himself but barely grazed the skin. Both murderer and victim were taken to the Shakespeare Tavern for urgent medical attention. Given the public nature of his crime, it didn't take long for Hackman to be tried for murder, and it took an even shorter time for him to be found guilty. In the dock Hackman described himself as 'the most wretched of human beings' and no one contradicted him. On 19 April, less than two weeks after murdering Martha Ray, the Reverend James Hackman was taken to Tyburn and hanged. The case was the talk of London, eliciting comment from such vaunted figures as Horace Walpole and Doctor Johnson. The case even inspired a hugely successful novel, *Love and Madness*, the following year. The unfortunate incumbent of Wiveton saw nothing of his fame – after a short clerical career spent coveting his neighbour's wife, engaging in adultery and, finally, committing murder, he ended up being publicly dissected for the benefit of medical students at the Royal College of Surgeons.

II

The Most Reverend and Right Honourable Lancelot Blackburne, Archbishop of York (1658–1743)

'His behaviour was never that expected of a cleric, indeed it was rarely that expected of a pirate'

There are many leaders in the history of the Church of England who were promoted due to their great holiness, their administrative skill or their inspirational leadership abilities. Lancelot Blackburne was not one of them. He is one of the most astonishing figures in the history of the Church, beginning his career as a pirate in the Caribbean and ending it as the second most senior clergyman in the country. Blackburne went up to Christ Church in 1676 and five years later was made a Deacon by the Bishop of Oxford. It was at this point that he mysteriously decided to go to the West Indies, spending most of his time on Nevis, an island known to be the operating centre for piracy against Spanish and French galleons. Exactly what Blackburne did there is not known. However, by the end of 1681 he was regularly being furnished with payments by the British Crown for 'secret services' – a poorly disguised seventeenth-century euphemism for privateering.

After three years in the Caribbean, clerical advancement beckoned. Blackburne returned to England, was ordained Priest and took up a series of sinecures in the Diocese of Exeter, conveniently far from serious oversight in London. He rose quickly and, even though as a Canon at Exeter he was briefly suspended for employing builders to construct a tunnel in order to enjoy late-night trysts with his neighbour's wife, eventually became Dean. There he might have remained were it not for the accession of George I. The womanising Hanoverian was on the lookout for a clergyman unscrupulous enough to marry him (bigamously) to his mistress. Blackburne was more than happy to do so, displaying remarkable pastoral flair when he counselled the incumbent Queen: 'Madam, I have been with your minister Walpole, and he tells me that you are a wise woman, and do not mind your husband's having a mistress.'

Blackburne's reward was to be made Bishop of Exeter and then, in 1724, Archbishop of York, a job he miraculously managed to keep for the next nineteen years. He neglected his duties, stopping any ordinations after his first few years in the post and refusing to conduct confirmations after an incident in Nottingham parish church. (Blackburne began the service but, having swiftly become bored, sent his servant to fetch him his pipe, some tobacco and a pint of ale to help pass the time. Such was the Vicar's fury that he forced the Archbishop out of the church with the words, 'No Archbishop shall make a tippling house of St Mary's so long as I am its Vicar'.) He didn't set aside his interest in women after his archiepiscopal appointment either. Horace Walpole recalled dining at Blackburne's London home in Downing Street (the home of many a rogue since) with his wife, his mistress Mrs Conwys and Thomas, his illegitimate son by a third woman, whom, in a show of paternal affection, he had made his Chaplain.

His trips to York were rare, but not wasted; on one visit he employed Dick Turpin as his butler and on another he was supposedly caught in what tabloid newspapers would now call 'a romp' involving, among others, a local milkmaid. It was said that, close to death, he mellowed somewhat, with the only remnant of his pirating past being his seraglio. Such were his carnal appetites that on his death a wit penned the lines, 'All the buxom damsels of the North,/ Who knew his parts, lament their going forth.'

Other contemporaries were kinder, Walpole calling him 'a gentleman to the last... [although] a man of this world'. Perhaps the best summing up of this extraordinary figure was that of the satirist William Donaldson, who remarked that his behaviour was seldom of a standard to be expected of a cleric; and seldom of a standard to be expected of a pirate.

III

The Very Reverend Marco de Dominis, Dean of Windsor and sometime Archbishop of Split (1560–1624)

'Odious both to God and to man'

Anglicanism is well-known within Christianity for its theological flexibility, but Marco Antonio de Dominis turned changing his mind into an art form. He was born Markantun Antun Domnianic on the island of Rab in present-day Croatia to a family of prominent local warlords. The Republic of Venice was, at this stage, emerging as the dominant Christian power on the fractious Balkan political scene, and so the young and ambitious Markantun undertook an education at the hands of the Jesuits in the Republic, changing his name to suit his new Latin masters and taking a job teaching mathematics at the great Venetian university in Padua.

He was seemingly destined for a university career when, in 1597, he was lured by the promise of patronage (a recurring theme) and persuaded by Cardinal Aldobrandini to abandon the Jesuits and take up the role of Bishop of Senj on the Croatian coast. Despite spending his tenure as Bishop unsuccessfully attempting to bribe local pirates to stop attacking the ships he had been using to trade with his supposed enemies, the Ottomans, de Dominis was so craven that he was still considered a safe bet as Archbishop of Split, and so, in 1602, he was promoted in the hope that he would continue his policy of spineless appeasement of the Pope. However, de Dominis had other ideas. In 1604, Rome ordered him to pay a percentage of his diocesan income to sustain a modest pension for the decrepit Dean of Udine. The Archbishop was furious at this enforced charity and so, in 1606, when the Republic of Venice and the Papacy fell out over who had the authority to arrest and try Priests, de

Dominis defected again and backed the Venetians with a series of vicious pamphlets directed at the Pope.

De Dominis fled to Venice where he lived under the protection of the Doge and continued to write thoroughly nasty things about Rome. However, by 1615 Venice needed Papal help against Spain and so, with the Inquisition circling, de Dominis arranged with James I's ambassador to flee to England and convert to Anglicanism. In the propaganda wars of the Reformation, the defection of a Roman Catholic Archbishop to the Church of England was a major coup. King James I quartered de Dominis with the Archbishop of Canterbury, and provided him with large sums of money to produce theological tracts denouncing the Papacy and extolling James's attempts at reunion of the Church.

However, in another recurring theme, it didn't take long for de Dominis to expend any goodwill he might have accrued. The Archbishop of Canterbury thought he was 'an ungrateful little beast' while other contemporary chroniclers thought him 'fat and pretentious'. He was passed from one institution to another as the Church of England desperately tried to find something to do with him. After being politely removed from Lambeth Palace, the universities of Oxford and Cambridge and from the houses of various lay hosts, he was eventually returned to the King who, still under the illusion that he could bring about the reunion of Christendom with the turncoat Archbishop by his side, made him Dean of Windsor. The Deanery came with minimal duties but an enormous salary that the King and various bishops helped top up by at least an extra £400 a year (worth just over £75,000 in today's money), yet this was not enough for the Dean. The Archbishop began to avoid the Dean and his constant whingeing about the paucity of his income, the lack of respect shown to him, the weather, indeed almost anything.

In the end, avarice proved to be his downfall. With an offer of 12,000 crowns a year and a Bishopric in Sicily on the table from Papal agents working in England, de Dominis manufactured an excuse about trying to broker reconciliation between Anglicans and Catholics and, as soon as he'd crossed the Channel (with several chests of money 'borrowed' from Windsor), he reconverted to Roman Catholicism. The Papacy, however, had learned to play the avaricious Archbishop at his own game. Following his arrival in Rome in 1623, he was seized by the Inquisition and died under house arrest a year later. The news was met with great enthusiasm in England, where he had been satirised early that year in Thomas Middleton's play *A Game of Chess* as a fat, gullible Bishop who falls under the sway of the Black Knight, the Machiavellian villain of the piece and a thinly veiled reference to the then Spanish ambassador. Perhaps the last words on the Dean of Windsor should go to his long-suffering handler, Archbishop George Abbott: 'He was a worldly man, without conscience or religion... odious both to God and to man.'

IV

The Reverend Dr Sir Robert Peat, Perpetual Curate of New Brentford (1772–1837)

The Brawling Knight and his Kleptomaniac Wife

Robert Peat was born in County Durham, the product of a union between an enterprising watchmaker and the daughter of once-powerful but now impoverished local gentry. This upbringing left him with something of a chip on his shoulder, and he spent an entire career neglecting his clerical duties in favour of bumping up his social and academic credentials by other means.

He was initially considered too dim-witted to go to university and so, for reasons not entirely clear, in 1790 he decided to take the equivalent of a gap year to Poland. There, apparently due to some act of service to the King, he was inducted into 'The Order of St Stanislaus'. The Polish decoration was the first in Peat's long-running collection of bizarre titles and the one he took most seriously. He spent much of the rest of his life trying to prove that he was in fact entitled to be addressed as 'Sir Robert', even though, four years after he'd been awarded the title, the Kingdom of Poland had ceased to exist. Eventually, at some point after 1790, Peat was awarded a 'ten-year degree' (an award abolished soon after for requiring 'no actual test of ability') at Trinity College, Cambridge, and, in 1794, was ordained. Not long after that, Peat approached the University of Glasgow to award him a doctorate. Despite his manifest lack of qualifications (and the fact that he was living in Biggleswade, Bedfordshire), they agreed, and he became, both ridiculously and indisputably, a Doctor of Divinity. (However, his long-running campaign to be recognised as a knight had gained very little traction.)

Despite his pretensions, Peat was clearly a charming man and managed to ingratiate himself with Regency society. In 1800, he was appointed a Chaplain to the Prince of Wales (despite never having met him) and used this position to gain, after four years of frantic letter-writing, a special licence from the (admittedly insane) King enabling him to wear the Order of St Stanislaus and to be addressed as 'Sir'.

This didn't help him when, in 1808, he got involved in a brawl outside the Theatre Royal on Drury Lane. Peat's insistence on being called 'Sir' had riled a man who, instead of paying him due deference, punched him. To add insult to injury, when Peat appeared in court over the incident, the lawyer defending also refused to call him 'Sir'. Peat protested that he would have produced the documentation proving his claim, only his house had been (conveniently) burgled and his insignia and paperwork stolen just a month before...

Not long after the theatre incident, Peat's behaviour turned increasingly erratic. Having finally attained his long-coveted knightly status, he became what a contemporary pamphlet referred to as 'proud, tyrannical and overbearing'. Still licking his wounds from the brawl and court humiliation, Peat set about a new course of action – he would find himself a wife. His fancy settled upon Jane Smith, an elderly kleptomaniac spinster who had been banned from a series of shops in Sunderland for hiding several pounds of butter in her petticoats. Despite being a confirmed miser, Smith also happened to be heiress to huge properties in Durham and a cousin of the Prince of Wales' secret wife, Mrs Fitzherbert, which might explain why Peat, now nearly overcome by gambling debts, found himself so attracted to her. After their marriage in 1815, they lived together in London for a short period until Peat caught his wife eating a mouldy pork pie in order to save money and decided enough was enough. He sent her back north, where she spent her days barging into other people's houses at mealtimes to avoid the expense of maintaining a cook. Peat visited her once a year, in order to ensure his cash flow.

After the marriage Peat found a new project: he decided to revive the Order of the Knights of Malta, with himself as Grand Prior. The Knights were a Roman Catholic order of crusading monks who had been dormant in England since the Reformation. In a flurry of enthusiasm, Peat spent vast sums of his wife's money procuring appropriate robes and arranging a lavish swearing-in ceremony (as well as threatening anyone who suggested it might not be a fantastic idea), only to receive cease and desist correspondence from the Order's extant representatives in Rome informing him that he was operating 'without any recognition' and that his Order was, in their eyes, illegal. Peat went ahead anyway, and the Order still exists in England today, albeit in the slightly modified format of the St John Ambulance first aid organisation.

Peat's triumph was short-lived. Only three years after making himself Grand Prior, he was dead. When his wife (by now in her nineties) received word that he had died she exclaimed that it was 'the best news I ever had in my life'. The miserly nonagenarian broke the habit of a lifetime and bought a bright yellow dress decorated in ostrich feathers. She proceeded to spend the day dancing through the streets of Sunderland singing 'Sir Robert is dead' by way of celebration. Although Peat died regretted by few who knew him, his wife's song would have afforded him some small comfort – she did, after all, refer to him by his proper title.

V

The Reverend James Stanier Clarke, Chaplain to the Prince of Wales (1767–1834)

The Divine and the Donkey

In common with many clergy during the Regency period, James Stanier Clarke did not feel himself bound to engage only with the propagation and practice of religion. In fact, he fancied himself as something of a polymath. Unfortunately, he turned out to be useless at almost everything. He was born on the island of Minorca where his father was Secretary to the British Governor. Eventually, James and his brother were sent to school in England and then went up to Cambridge. Edward, James's younger brother, excelled, first being ordained Priest and then obtaining a role first as university librarian, then as Professor of Mineralogy, ending his career in a blaze of glory by helping to perfect the gas blowpipe. James, by contrast, was booted out without completing his degree.

Despite his academic failure, Clarke was ordained and ended up as Vicar of a quiet suburb of Brighton. This enterprise didn't last long either – he found funerals too distressing and so, after two years in the post, he moved on again. Having established that he was suited neither to university nor parish work, James took advantage of his father's contacts and became a naval Chaplain on a patrol vessel in the English Channel.

Very little patrolling can have been done, or at least, if it was, it was done without the aid of the Chaplain, as James spent most of his time in London where, in 1799, he met the Prince Regent. The Prince, perhaps impressed to see a waistline as burgeoning as his own (Clarke was, if contemporary portraits are anything to go by, enormous), appointed him as his personal Chaplain and librarian.

Clarke was now technically in charge of the moral welfare of the household of the most debauched man in Western Europe. Needless to say, he failed miserably. In 1813, while the Prince's household was staying with Lord Egremont at Petworth House in Sussex, Clarke was caught arranging a night-time tryst with a housemaid. Later that evening, the Earl threw a ball to celebrate the defeat of Napoleon at the

Battle of Leipzig, at which Clarke consumed a staggeringly large quantity of alcohol. While Clarke was downstairs toasting victory, the Prince's friends procured a donkey from the Earl's estate, somehow contrived to dress it in a housemaid's petticoat and put it into the bibulous Chaplain's bed, where it lay concealed until a hugely intoxicated Clarke heaved himself onto the mattress next to it. At this point the donkey awoke with a start and, clearly perturbed by the enormous pink blob that had suddenly appeared next to it, began to bray and kick with gusto, catapulting the unfortunate clergyman out of bed with almighty force. The incident highly amused the Prince Regent but scandalised the nation, not least when a satirical print, *The Divine and the Donkey*, began to be circulated around London.

Accepting that his moral authority had evaporated, Clarke turned his attention to his role as librarian, having been awarded the title 'Historiographer Royal' the year before (despite an attempt by the Poet Laureate to veto his appointment on account of his being 'a most extraordinary blockhead'). Clarke began to fancy himself as a man of letters and invited authors such as Walter Scott and Jane Austen to come and see the Prince's Library. After persuading Austen to dedicate her novel *Emma* to the Prince Regent, Clarke went one step further, writing her letters full of suggestions about how she might improve her style and suggesting various plots for novels, including sketching out the character of a potential hero for her next novel – a clergyman with naval experience, who was in the service of a Prince...

Austen responded with the biting satirical piece, *Plan of a Novel, according to Hints from Various Quarters*, and, once again, Clarke's ambitions fell away in the face of mockery. But when the Prince Regent became King George IV in 1820, he did not forget his old Chaplain. In the face of opposition from the prime minister and the Archbishop of Canterbury, he managed to get Clarke made a Canon of Windsor. There he stayed, writing articles about famous shipwrecks, until he died in 1834. Clarke was a chancer and a fool but it's hard not to feel a smidgeon of affection for the man. He is, perhaps, best summed up by the epitaph he penned for himself: 'He was no man's enemy – except his own.'

VI

The Reverend Bruce Cornford,
Vicar of St Matthew's, Southsea (1867–1940)

The Portsmouth Priest with a Need for Speed

For many people the life of a Vicar is synonymous with a quiet, safe, stately existence, but not many people know about the bizarre career of Bruce Cornford. Born of a clerical family, it was perhaps unsurprising that Cornford took Holy Orders as well; what was surprising was his conduct after his ordination.

His clerical career didn't have the most auspicious of beginnings. Having just been made a Deacon, Cornford was sent to serve his curacy in Portsmouth. The Vicar who was meant to be training him was laid-back, when he wasn't away on holiday. After being left alone to run the parish for a prolonged period while the incumbent was on the continent, Cornford finally cracked and, in protest at these regular absences, put his superior's house on the market. When the Vicar was glancing over the English newspapers some time later, he happened to notice a sizeable Portsmouth residence up for sale. His interest piqued, he read on, only to realise to his horror that it was his own house that was being flogged to the highest bidder. The 'all enquiries to Rev. Bruce Cornford' part of the advert rather gave the game away – the Vicar cut short his jaunt and Cornford got the sack.

Undeterred, Cornford set about raising money to build his own church and, having somehow secured both the funding and the Bishop's permission, in 1904 he became Vicar of a new parish – St Matthew's in Southsea. Under his own steam, Cornford could focus on his real interests. At first he tried to get involved in politics; however, after he encouraged a group of local suffragettes to throw bricks through the windows of Portsmouth Post Office, he decided to keep a lower profile. Cornford turned his attention instead to thrill-seeking.

Cornford was particularly fascinated by vehicles that crashed easily, such as planes and motorbikes. He quickly made friends with leading figures in the nascent world of flight, including Sir Sefton Brancker, head of the Royal Aero Club's racing committee. Soon Cornford was using the oratory skills polished in the pulpit to tour aviation clubs and fundraising dinners, speaking in favour of establishing competitive aeroplane racing as well as advocating, among other things, that flying licences be doled out to ordinary citizens. Cornford's search for adrenaline led to him founding a motorcycle club specialising in 'road runs' where the Vicar of St Matthew's and his companions would tear along the country's side roads at great speed, to the horror of his parishioners and other motorists alike.

Cornford's love of high-octane activity was matched only by his loathing of any pastime he thought dull. He developed a particular hatred for philately, writing a long and rambling piece in his parish magazine about how well these 'tiny fragments of paper' would burn in Hell. He began using the seemingly innocuous platform of the magazine to push his other various causes – from his bizarre personal enmity towards the Archbishop of Canterbury (a man, according to Cornford, 'not fit to lead the Mothers' Union across Southsea Common') to his hatred of his ecumenical colleagues (he referred to the Roman Catholic Church in England as 'an Italian mission to the Irish'). As a result, the magazine developed a cult following, as people waited to see on which subject the Vicar would hold forth next. Buoyed by this interest, he soon indulged his old political yen, predicting in 1934 that Adolf Hitler would prove to be nothing more than 'hot air'.

Cornford remained Vicar of St Matthew's (promotion was not forthcoming) until his death in 1940. Barely a year after he died, the church that Cornford had spent so much effort building and which he had served for almost his entire career was gone. Ironically, given the Vicar's aeronautical obsession and his personal predictions for Germany, St Matthew's was reduced to a shell by the Luftwaffe.

VII

The Reverend Harold Davidson, Rector of Stiffkey (1875–1937)

The Tabloid Daniel in the Lions' Den

One would be hard-pressed to find a more tragi-comic figure in the history of English public life than the Rector of Stiffkey. For a brief period in the 1930s, Harold Davidson was the most famous clergyman in the world, his legal entanglements with the Diocese of Norwich discussed from New York to Nanking. The story of how Davidson went from being the parson of a small Norfolk parish to being eaten by a lion on the seafront at Skegness is one of the most extraordinary in the annals of the Church of England.

Harold Davidson had always juggled two vocations – to the Priesthood and to the theatre. During his time as an undergraduate at Oxford, he spent most of his time in amateur dramatic productions. However, a combination of family pressure and spiritual yearning led Davidson to seek Holy Orders, and in 1906 he became the Rector of Stiffkey in North Norfolk. But the lure of the bright lights was too much for Davidson and he began to spend almost the entire week in London, only returning to Stiffkey on Saturday night or early Sunday morning. His flair for the dramatic had earned him the post of Chaplain to various theatres and he spent the week bustling between them, ministering to the show business community. It didn't escape comment that Davidson invariably judged chorus girls and struggling actresses to be most in need of pastoral attention. After certain trips to London, the Rector would bring whole groups of out-of-work young actresses back to Stiffkey for pyjama parties at the rectory, much to the consternation of his parishioners (and, indeed, his wife). As one biographer put it, 'His downfall was girls. Not a girl, not five or six girls even, not a hundred, but the entire tremulous universe of girlhood. Shingled heads, clear cheeky eyes, nifty legs, warm, blunt-fingered workaday hands, small firm breasts and, most importantly, good strong healthy teeth, besotted him.'

After the First World War, Davidson intensified his activities and, with the new, self-appointed title of 'the Prostitutes' Padre' he set about helping as many girls as he could. There is little suggestion that Davidson ever sought anything from these women; his pastoral 'help' invariably meant giving them money for rent and taking them out to a Lyons' Corner House for afternoon tea. That said, it was clear that Davidson increasingly believed his own fantasies – he would often claim that he had links to Hollywood stars and was banned from a number of tea shops after attempting to 'help' the waitresses there as well. On top of this, he had also fallen victim to an American con man who convinced him he had links with the New York Stock Exchange.

By the late 1920s, Davidson was bankrupt and on increasingly thin ice as he repeatedly missed services while arranging theatrical jobs for his girls in London. After a series of complaints, the Bishop of Norwich decided to take action. Normally Diocesan Consistory Courts deal with the moving of church ornaments or occasional financial irregularities – hardly the stuff of tabloid gossip columns – but Davidson's hearing was attended by huge crowds. A series of actresses, dancing girls and waitresses essentially confirmed the same narrative: Davidson was an exceptionally strange man, but he had not done anything that could count as serious misconduct. Meanwhile, Davidson himself refused to acknowledge that anything was wrong – when the Bishop sent a young clergyman to stand in for the Rector one Sunday morning, Davidson ran into the service and proceeded to wrestle with the cleric until they were pulled apart by a Churchwarden. Newspapers from London, Paris and New York sent teams of reporters to the sleepy Norfolk hamlet each Sunday to see what would happen next. Eventually the prosecution found the evidence they needed: a photograph of Davidson with a naked showgirl. It is arguable that the encounter was staged in order to put Davidson in a compromising position, but it was enough to convict him and, in July, Davidson was, to use an apposite word, defrocked.

Naturally, Davidson refused to accept the judgement and decided to pursue the matter in the secular courts. There was one problem, though; he now had no income whatsoever. So, following his first vocation, Davidson returned to the theatre or, to be more precise, to variety shows. He went first to Wimbledon and then to Blackpool where, such was his fame, hundreds would turn out to see the Rector of Stiffkey. His bizarre shows largely consisted of him reading out sermons while sitting in a barrel. He made periodic attempts to return to his church – in August 1932 he preached to a crowd of over 1,000 people outside the building, while his parishioners desperately tried to pretend he wasn't there. At one appearance he approached a Churchwarden and demanded to be given a set of keys to the church. The Churchwarden responded by picking up the diminutive cleric, turning him round and booting him hard on the behind.

After this Davidson returned disconsolately to his barrel. He decided that his act needed something to spice it up. He experimented with freezing himself in an enormous glass-fronted refrigerator unit, as well as being roasted in a replica of a gas oven, while being poked by a robot dressed as Satan. In 1937, tired of having to share a billing with acts such as 'Mariana the Gorilla Girl' and 'The World's Fattest Man', Davidson began performing at Skegness, which he considered less 'vulgar' than Blackpool. Again, looking to keep his act both fresh and classy, Davidson decided to bill himself as a modern Daniel in the lions' den. Old habits die hard and, rather than choosing a hardened circus trainer to help with his act, Davidson's two lions, Freddie and Toto, were under the control of an attractive sixteen-year-old girl. It was, perhaps, not very surprising when, on 28 July 1937, after Davidson had entered the ring and shouted at him, Freddie the lion broke free from his young tamer and, in front of a large crowd, began to eat the former Rector of Stiffkey.

Davidson took two days to die of his injuries. His bizarre career and even stranger death attracted headlines, books and even, appropriately, a stage musical. The Church of England eventually admitted it had been a little hard on the Rector and agreed to pay his wife and children a pension after his death. After the incident on Skegness seafront, even his parishioners relented and paid for him to be buried in the churchyard. Visitors to Stiffkey today can see the last earthly resting place of the well-meaning little clergyman from Norfolk who, for a short time, could claim to be one of the most famous men in the world.

VIII

The Reverend Sir Henry Bate-Dudley, Rector of Willingham (1745–1824)

The Fighting Parson

There can have been few clerics in history less temperamentally suited to the clerical 'meek and mild' stereotype than Henry Bate-Dudley. Born the second son of a clergyman, he went up to Oxford but paid little or no attention to his studies and failed to get a degree. By 1772, he had followed his father into Holy Orders and was appointed Curate at Hendon. However, the lure of London was too tempting and he dedicated most of his time to getting ahead in society.

Through his societal connections, Bate-Dudley was linked to the famous actress Mrs Hartley (although he ended up marrying her sister). One Friday evening in July 1773, he was accompanying the actress on 'a walk' around Vauxhall Gardens (not a place renowned for nocturnal salubriousness) when a group of young men led by a soldier on leave, one Captain Crofts, began looking at her in a way that the clergyman objected to. Bate-Dudley went over and accosted them, calling the group 'impudent puppies'; the fight escalated, with observers commenting on the astonishing range of coarse language deployed by the parson until, in a fit of rage, Bate-Dudley demanded that they settle the affair with a fight. Captain Crofts accepted and a match was set for the following afternoon in the back room of the Turk's Head pub on the Strand. When the time came, Crofts, having seen Bate-Dudley limbering up for the sparring match (he was described as 'a tight made fellow, capable of bruising'), decided that he would apologise after all. His companion Captain Miles, however, was less conciliatory and agreed to step into his place and fight the well-built clergyman instead. It was a decision he probably regretted – contemporary press reports described the event as 'a fair set to', in which Miles failed to lay a single blow on the parson and ended up being sent home in a carriage having had 'his face turned into jelly'.

The incident made Bate-Dudley's name in society, which was furthered by his appointment to the editorship of the *Morning Post* – a gossip sheet not dissimilar to the contemporary *Hello!* magazine. It was while there that he sealed his reputation as 'the fighting parson'. Having written a savagely rude article about the Countess of Strathmore, he was challenged to retract his comments by a supporter of hers called Andrew Stoney. When (as was inevitable) the pugnacious parson refused, Stoney challenged him to a duel with pistols. Bate-Dudley accepted and won, although fortunately for his career – and perhaps unfortunately for the Church of England – he did stop short of killing him. Despite being prepared to fight a duel on behalf of the publication, by 1780 Bate-Dudley had fallen out with the *Morning Post* and was sacked, but not before he had challenged the magazine's proprietor to yet another duel, during which the clergyman shot the unfortunate press magnate in the arm. With money earned from succeeding his father as Rector of the rich parish of North Fambridge, Bate-Dudley set up a new publication, the imaginatively named *Morning Herald*, as a direct rival.

The *Herald* was a short-lived exercise; within six months of its first edition, its owner/editor was in prison. Bate-Dudley had finally baited the wrong man and, after writing a vicious article about the Duke of Richmond, found himself in the dock on charges of libel. He lost and was imprisoned for twelve months. While in gaol, cognisant that finding work as a clergyman might be a little tricky after his parole, Bate-Dudley cunningly bought the right to 'present' a Vicar to the parish of Bradwell-juxta-Mare in Essex and, when its aged incumbent finally died, promptly appointed himself to the role. Perhaps unsurprisingly, the Church wasn't overly pleased about this and sued Bate-Dudley for simony. After a protracted legal case, which he financed by writing bawdy musical entertainments for theatres around Covent Garden, the courts eventually found against Bate-Dudley and so he moved to Ireland where he spent the next eight years in the most almighty sulk as Vicar of several villages near Wexford.

His bucolic surroundings and his advanced age (he was by now in his sixties) mellowed Bate-Dudley and in 1812 he returned to England to become Rector of Willingham in Cambridgeshire. Here he lived a calm life, although he was fond of hunting; at one point he chased a fox onto the roof of his church and then climbed up after it with a hound under each arm to finish the job. He was even made a baronet for his services as a magistrate in 1813. By the end he had become a positively respectable figure, although some of the old fighting spirit remained – in 1816, when a group of rioters in Ely armed themselves and fired on the local militia, Bate-Dudley (who, at seventy-one, had been made a Canon of the cathedral) rallied the troops, leading them in a charge to flush out the rioters. When he died eight years later, he was mourned across several counties. His career was undoubtedly a diverse one, perhaps best summed up by Dr Johnson, who considered him to have had 'great courage' but found that, as a clergyman, he was 'of no merit' whatsoever.

IX

The Honourable and Reverend William Capel, Vicar of Watford (1775–1854)

Bribery, Booze and Brushes with the Law – the Bookies' favourite Vicar

William Capel was the archetype of that particular type of English rogue – a cad. Interested almost exclusively in his own pleasure, he was a pre-eminent huntsman, womaniser and drinker. He was also, for a total of fifty-five years, responsible for the souls of the good people of Watford. In

fairness he was rather forced into a clerical career – his elder brother, the Earl of Essex, lived up the road and wanted
his feckless younger sibling close at hand so as to be able
to curtail any misbehaviour. The Earl's plan was a manifest
failure, as William spent most of his time away playing
cricket for the recently formed Marylebone Cricket Club
(MCC). When he did return to Watford, it was almost
always to hunt foxes. After a few years of incumbency, he
decided to employ a Curate in order to give him more free
time on Sundays (the day he customarily toured his parish
blocking up foxholes in order to make Monday's hunting
a little easier). It was over this pastime that William eventually fell foul of his brother. In 1809, William was, as was
his custom, out hunting. He was at the front of the pack
when the fox he was chasing dived for cover in land owned
by his brother. Despite the gates to his sibling's estate being
locked, William jumped over the fence and encouraged his
hounds to smash through after him. The resultant damage
enraged the Earl, who took his brother to court. Given that
the Vicar's actions were a clear instance of trespass, his
chances were never especially bright, but they worsened
when it transpired that he'd tried to bribe his brother's
gamekeeper by offering him a barrel of ale. William lost
the case and, more importantly, his main protector against
the nefarious forces that seemed intent on making him do
his job.

Capel was notorious for prioritising a boozy lunch over
his parish duties – once knocking off an entire service in
just nine minutes in anticipation of his pre-prandial bottle
of sherry. If he had a large party waiting he would routinely
cancel communion services altogether. He went too far,
however, when, in 1829, he accidentally double-booked a
funeral and a particularly bibulous lunch party. After the

coffin and mourners had been kept waiting some time, a worried Churchwarden dared to venture over to the Vicarage to remind the parson that he was needed, only to be met with the slurred response, 'I wouldn't leave my dinner even if I was burying a Saint'. Regrettably for Capel, the woman he was meant to be burying was something rather more formidable: the mistress of a Cabinet minister who, furious at the Vicar's conduct, reported him to his Bishop.

The Bishop suspended Capel and appointed a Curate to take his place, with the instruction that the Vicar pay the replacement clergyman out of his own pocket. Capel refused to pay the poor man and, to make matters worse, would interrupt his services. Given that he had shown practically no interest in his parish prior to his suspension, Capel's newfound enthusiasm for ministry was little short of miraculous. On one memorable occasion, he appeared fully robed at the start of the service, and then raced the unfortunate Curate down the aisle in order to get to the pulpit first. Capel, having learned from his previous brush with the law, dragged the disciplinary action out for a full three years until, in 1832, after the Bishop had spent huge amounts of money trying to get rid of him, he succeeded in getting the complaint dismissed on a technicality.

The Bishop was, understandably, somewhat vexed a few years later when it transpired that a charity sermon he was preaching was to be delivered in St Mary's, Watford. Capel deliberately made the Bishop feel uncomfortable, insisting on wearing an ancient dressing gown and a pair of bright red slippers to meet him. Capel's charm must have won out, though, as by the time the Bishop left they were – in Capel's own words – 'great friends'. Despite no evidence of any reform to his behaviour, no further action was taken and, in a final twist, sixty years after the almighty row between

Bishop and Vicar, Capel's great-granddaughter married the Bishop's grandson.

X

The Reverend Dr Edward Drax Free, Rector of All Saints, Sutton (1764–1843)

'Almost anyone would be remembered as a Saint in comparison to Edward Drax Free'

The marvellously named Edward Drax Free has the distinction of being – and the author writes this advisedly – probably the most troublesome clergyman in the history of the Church of England. Free went up to St John's College, Oxford, where he almost immediately began to exhibit signs of uncooperative and destructive behaviour. He was considered to be one of the most impressive drinkers in Oxford (a famously well-lubricated university), and routinely caused considerable damage to college property as well as to himself and others during his marathon binges. Despite (or perhaps because of) this debauchery, he was initially respected in St John's: he was made a fellow in 1784 and ordained not long after. These new responsibilities in no way affected Free's behaviour – if anything it got worse. In one of his many disciplinary hearings for drunken behaviour, Free decided that the best way to redeem himself in the eyes of the college authorities was to interrupt proceedings by punching the bursar in the face. Eventually even a college as lax as St John's had had enough and, in 1808, they hastily arranged for Free to be inflicted on the unfortunate villagers of Sutton in Bedfordshire as their new Rector.

After much complaining, Free arrived in Sutton in the October of that year and almost immediately set to work building a reputation by impregnating his housekeeper. It soon became clear that Free had absolutely no intention of attending to his parish whatsoever. He spent the vast majority of his time wandering around his rectory in a dressing gown, cataloguing the enormous collection of French pornography he had brought with him, occasionally showing it to anyone unfortunate enough to call on him during daylight hours. He kept the church building locked most of the time in order to disabuse any possible illusion on the part of the villagers that he might actually lead a service. On the rare occasion that he did turn up, he invariably did so hungover and with the sole purpose of extorting cash from his hapless congregation.

Money was a major issue for Free. Heavy drinking, womanising, gambling and porn collecting are expensive hobbies and even his generous clerical stipend proved insufficient. The first official complaint about him was made after he decided to convert the village churchyard into a private farm. If they wanted to get to church, villagers had to run a gauntlet of enraged cattle and the scattered remains of recently buried loved ones that had been dug up by Free's large herd of pigs. The Archdeacon, perhaps mindful of what had happened to the bursar of St John's, was reluctant to discipline Free and timidly suggested that Free affix rings to the noses of the pigs to make them easier to catch.

Emboldened by this weak diocesan response, Free decided to go several steps further, first arranging for every oak tree in the parish (whether it was technically on Church land or not) to be cut down and flogged for timber. One Sunday the few remaining members of the congregation arrived for morning service only to find the church without a roof. It transpired that the Rector had arranged for the lead to be stripped and sold to a scrap metal merchant to cover his gambling debts. Free continued to defy any attempt to discipline him. When he wasn't collecting dirty pictures or stripping the parish of its assets he was almost always arguing with someone. From the man employed to clear the church drains (whose tools Free hid in a fit of pique) to his own church council (whom he would only talk to once a year outdoors), almost nobody was safe.

It was as a result of one of these feuds that Free finally got his comeuppance. Free's confrontation with the squire of the village, Sir Montague Burgoyne, had begun five years earlier in 1817. Free had been undertaking one of his periodic money-making schemes – in this case suing various people for not attending church (despite the fact that it was roofless and almost permanently closed) under obscure clauses in the anti-Roman Catholic Acts passed by Elizabeth I more than two hundred years earlier. Free claimed that Burgoyne owed him £360 for non-attendance, a figure conveniently similar to the outstanding debts that Free had accrued in the previous year. The case was heard and swiftly rejected after the defence pointed out that, firstly, Burgoyne wasn't a Roman Catholic and so the law didn't apply and, secondly, that Free hadn't put on any services on the days he had accused Burgoyne of staying at home. Burgoyne decided to revenge himself and in 1823 began legal proceedings to get Free deprived of his living. The Rector successfully managed to evade prosecution for seven years, despite the parish of Sutton (and the Bishop) supporting Burgoyne. He employed numerous diversionary tactics, weaving an impressively complex legal web that saw the case taken all the way to the House of Lords.

Eventually, in 1830, Free's luck ran out. The Bishop of Lincoln sent a party to remove Free from the rectory and reclaim its contents. In the event, there was very little left to reclaim as Free had sold most church property and used the rest to barricade himself in; armed with two pistols and fortified by the attentions of his favourite serving girl, Free prepared for a showdown. After a number of shots were fired, the Bishop's men decided their best approach was to lay siege and starve the Rector out. Some sympathetic farm labourers who appreciated Free's rustic use of language and somewhat unconventional management style smuggled him some food. However, after two weeks, he had drunk all of his claret and, facing the very real prospect of sobriety, Free gave up.

Having been ejected from Sutton, Free turned his attention to his old college. He spent the next thirteen years trying to force St John's to restore him to his fellowship. His efforts came to an abrupt end in 1843 when, having just exited a tavern (where else?) on Gray's Inn Lane, Free was hit by a cart and killed. Free may well have been 'a disgrace to himself, his college and the Church' but he cannot be totally forgotten – the legacy of his escapades remains with the Church of England today in the form of the Church Discipline Act of 1840, brought in to stop anyone even remotely like the Reverend Dr Edward Drax Free from ever holding office again.

A GLOSSARY

of Terms Clerical and
Ecclesiological for the General
Benefit of the Reader

Anglicanism – A tradition within the worldwide Church derived from the Church of England. Represented in the global Anglican Communion, a motley collection of Christians who were mostly the offspring of that Church's missionary efforts. Now all they have in common is a small assortment of hymns, sherry addiction, and mutual loathing.

✠ ✠ ✠

Archbishop – The senior cleric in charge of a large group of dioceses, known as a province. In England there are two, Canterbury and York, who have been bickering about which is technically more senior since the Dark Ages. Formerly, the Archbishops were two of the most powerful men in the land, whereas today their primary purpose is to look decorative at royal events, pretend they don't hate their fellow guests on breakfast television, and avoid breaking wind at state banquets.

Archdeacon – Not, as you might have thought, some sort of super-deacon. Rather, these figures are in charge of the nitty-gritty, day-to-day management of ecclesiastical affairs. Their role is varied, including stopping Bishops stepping out of line and ensuring that the Church of England remains focused on its primary purpose – namely keeping several thousand of the nation's most ancient buildings standing using only the proceeds of a Sunday School cake sale and the fifteen half shillings Beryl from the WI found down the back of her sofa. They are also in charge of clergy discipline, a role which, as this collection shows, they only very rarely have to perform...

✠ ✠ ✠

Bishop – A group of men (and now, after some, ahem, wrangling, women too) who are waiting for one of the Archbishops to retire/resign/die so that they might fill their spot. In the meantime they are allowed out by their Archdeacons for limited periods to perform acts of service within the community, such as the opening of church lavatory facilities and raising spirits in communities that have lost sight of their purpose and hope, such as the House of Lords.

✠ ✠ ✠

Canon – A title associated with a cathedral. Technically it comes with a 'stall', giving the cleric the right to sit in the best part of the building, i.e. nearer to the Bishop. There are two types: Residentiary Canons, who are given a nice house and a job at the cathedral in return for not saying nasty things about the Dean in public; and Honorary Canons, who are given a nice title in return for not saying nasty things about their lack of pension in public.

Chaplain – A cleric who has, inexplicably, got fed up of the wranglings of the Church of England and so is employed in a ministry role by a secular institution. Places that attract applications from clergy desperate to find a position outside the parish include infectious disease wards, Luton airport, and HMP Broadmoor.

✟ ✟ ✟

Church of England, The – an organisation that seeks to put into practice the transformative message of Jesus Christ via the medium of jumble sales, bad coffee and emotional stuntedness. This strategy has, until recently, proved a remarkably effective one among the English people.

✟ ✟ ✟

Curate – A junior cleric who serves a period of training under a more senior Priest at the start of their ministry. A curacy is a little like an apprenticeship but without the acquisition of practical skills and with a higher chance of developing gout.

✟ ✟ ✟

Deacon – The first (along with Priest and Bishop) of the three orders of Sacred Ministry in the Church. From the Greek διάκονος – meaning 'dogsbody'– Deacons are committed to proclaiming the Gospel and performing acts of mercy. These include visiting the sick, helping the poor, tea runs, photocopying, etc. For most clergy the role of Deacon is a stepping stone to being made a Priest and so, after a year, they can forget about such trifles as serving others for perpetuity.

Dean – A distinctly slippery term (often occupied by correspondingly slippery individuals) with several different meanings.

1. *In a Cathedral.*

Here the Dean is the senior cleric and technically in charge of the entire building and its assets, a monarch of all they survey. Consequently, it is their fault when things go wrong (such as budget deficits, accidental iconoclasm, undeserving individuals crushed by falling masonry etc.) However, there is some ambiguity as to the order of precedence in cathedrals and so, when things go right (such as budget surpluses, deliberate iconoclasm, deserving individuals crushed by falling masonry, etc.) they are considered junior to the Bishop.

2. *At Cambridge.*

As befits a university founded by churchmen, Deans at Cambridge colleges are ordained figures with a major role in college life. Their primary duties are the maintenance of the college chapel and the decimation of the college wine cellar.

3. *At Oxford.*

Deans at Oxford are figures who ensure the punishment of wickedness and vice, uphold good standards of behaviour and discourage the excesses of drinking culture in a particular college. As such, it is a position to which most clergy are temperamentally unsuited.

✠ ✠ ✠

Diocese – A geographical area made up of a large number of parishes and run by a Bishop. Also the name for the administrative body that oversees that area. As with the regional head office of any secular company or a district HQ of a political party, this oversight mostly manifests itself in the issuing of deliberately unattainable targets and the repetition of slogans which will have to be changed within the month when someone notices a spelling mistake on the publicity material.

✠ ✠ ✠

High Church – The wing of the Church primarily concerned with dressing up. Historically the 'Cavalier' party of the Church, but it suffered something of a continental infection (known as Roman fever) in the mid-nineteenth century and has never really recovered. Keen on lace, ritual and gin. Not keen on doing what Bishops tell them to.

✠ ✠ ✠

Low Church – The wing of the Church primarily concerned with dressing down. Historically the 'Puritan' party of the Church but suffered an outbreak of charisma in the mid-twentieth century and has never really recovered. Keen on repeating song lyrics, the Bible, repeating song lyrics, and hand waving. Even less keen on doing what Bishops tell them to.

✠ ✠ ✠

Methodists – A sect who were asked to leave the Church of England in the eighteenth century for singing too loudly and talking about God too much. Once a populous breed in Britain, they are now sadly diminished since the death of their Grand Mufti, Dame Thora Hird. Methodism's combination of misplaced optimism and teetotal lifestyle is still very popular in America and Africa whereas in this country these are now only adhered to (and then, grudgingly) during the month of January.

Parish – The most basic geographical and administrative unit in the Church. Technically every inch of England is covered by a Church of England parish, meaning that the member of the clergy in charge has 'cure of souls' of every person who lives there, whether they tick a box on a census form or not. On top of this the parish will have at least one (often crumbling) building as well as a myriad of committees and associated organisations whose purpose is to make life easier for the incumbent by bombarding them with requests, complaints and demands. Fortunately, the Priest is obliged to live in their parish and so can be accessed at any hour of the day by anyone who lives there. Truly a vision of peaceful bliss.

✠ ✠ ✠

Priest – The second order of clergy and by far the most numerous. Clergy are ordained as a Priest by the Bishop which puts them in the line of succession to Jesus himself, and enables them to celebrate the sacred mystery of Holy Communion, a gift imparted by the Holy Ghost. Ordination does not, however, impart any skills in rudimentary accountancy, lavatory repair or in how to deal with some of the lunatics who call the Church home.

✠ ✠ ✠

Quakers – A sect who were asked to leave the Church of England in the seventeenth century during an argument over oat-based breakfast cereal. They instead pursued a mode of worship that mostly involved sitting in silence waiting for someone to say something, a bit like a prolonged ice-breaking exercise. They became famous for their high standards of behaviour and commitment to public service, producing such luminaries as the Cadbury family,

Elizabeth Fry and that titan of twentieth-century morality, Richard Nixon.

✠ ✠ ✠

Rector – An intruding minister who spends a couple of years inflicting their poor taste and interminable sermons on another parish before moving on, allowing the laity to clear up the mess and then continue in their habits as if nothing had happened.

✠ ✠ ✠

Roman Catholicism – The true, uninterrupted continuation of one of the most significant ideas in history – the Roman Imperial cult. The single most adhered-to faith in the world apart from, if Professor Dawkins is to be believed, atheism (which is the default intellectual position of newborn children, toadstools, the chlamydia virus, etc.). As befits such a diverse and complex global institution, its operation is entirely vested in a solitary pensioner squatting in an art gallery.

✠ ✠ ✠

Vicar – Exactly the same as a Rector but with, historically, a lower pay packet. Now, in the interests of fairness, both are paid as poorly as each other.

APPENDIX

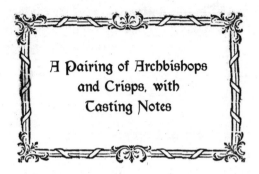

A Pairing of Archbishops
and Crisps, with
Tasting Notes

How the idea of pairing those august occupants of St Augustine's throne with crisps first came to lodge itself in my frontal lobe, I couldn't say. It is said writers should write about what interests them and so, as a clergyman of the Church of England, and one with a passing interest in the past, I feel it's in my professional interest to keep an eye on the boss (at least the one on earth) and his predecessors. As for crisps, well, they are almost always on my mind. I adore them in every one of their forms and they bring me unbridled pleasure. The packet torn open and shared on the pub table, the handful grabbed to render the official function more bearable, the solitary morsel enjoyed crunch by satisfying crunch – all these are signs that there is some residual good in the postlapsarian order after all. Therefore, I suppose it was only a matter of time before these two subjects elided within my consciousness. Below is a definitive pairing, from Thomas Cranmer to Rowan Williams, of Archbishops and crisps.

Rowan Williams – Thai Sweet Chilli Sensations

Complex and with clear Eastern influences, Rowan is the flagship flavour of the Sensations range. Yes, it's the sort of crisp you could take to Cambridge high table, but it's also a crisp with an air of dark, Dostoevskian mystery, too.

✠ ✠ ✠

George Carey – Twiglets

A crisp with a solid working-class pedigree. Twiglets saw a spike in popularity in the nineties, but now they're likely to be an opinion divider if brought up at a dinner party or the General Synod of the Church of England.

✠ ✠ ✠

Robert Runcie – Wotsits

Now, you think of the Wotsit as an airy crisp with little sub-stance, but next thing you know it's delivered a big flavour hit, wound up Mrs Thatcher, and shot a man in the Second World War. And you're left with orangey fingers, wondering how you misjudged it.

✠ ✠ ✠

APPENDIX

Donald Coggan – Mini Cheddars

It's easy to mock the Mini Cheddar, the safe, suburban pair of hands of the crisp world, but what other snack can you serve across social situations, to Catholic and Methodist alike? All hail this stolid lunch-box morale booster!

✠ ✠ ✠

Michael Ramsey – Skips

The Skip should not work as a crisp. It's made of tapioca and is the flavour of a horrible seventies dinner party starter – yet it's one of the jewels of the crisp crown, with hidden depths of fizz and flavour lurking in each tapioca crevice/chapter of its published work.

✠ ✠ ✠

Geoffrey Fisher – McCoy's Flame Grilled Steak

There's no messing about with Steak McCoy's. If there were any crisp that would be able to plan a coronation, hold very questionable views on nuclear war, and revive a flagging national institution, it'd be this one.

✠ ✠ ✠

William Temple – Bacon Fries

A crisp for a time of need. The sort of crisp that you reach for after a few pints and let its delicious saltiness fill you with inspiration for a vision of the postwar welfare state. The only problem is they're always gone too soon.

✠ ✠ ✠

Cosmo Gordon Lang – Pringles

A confident and imperious crisp, the Pringle sits in its tower and it judges you. It watches from the buffet at your work Xmas do and judges you as you try to dance/attempt to marry an American divorcee. And most regrettably of all, deep down, you know that its judgement is right.

✠ ✠ ✠

Randall Davidson – Pom-Bears

First and foremost, Randall Davidson is the successor to Augustine who bears the closest physical resemblance to a Pom-Bear. Their aerated potato faces carry a sense of strange ursine melancholy, one reflected in portraits of the unfortunate Archbishop. If a crisp were going to resign after failing to revise the Prayer Book, it would be this one.

✠ ✠ ✠

Frederick Temple – Frazzles

As everyone knows, the Frazzle is merely a prototype, surpassed by its more impressive offspring, the Bacon Fry. Yet, without the slightly passé, rough-round-the-edge Frazzle, we'd be without its only begotten pub stalwart, and for that it deserves our thanks.

✠ ✠ ✠

Edward White Benson – Scampi 'n' Lemon Nik Naks

If you told someone you wanted to market a crisp containing actual fish, they'd look at you as if you were mad. As they would if you wanted to make a schoolteacher obsessed with the idea of ghosts dragging people to their deaths Archbishop of Canterbury. Joshua 21:45 – 'all came to pass.'

✠ ✠ ✠

Archibald Campbell Tait – French Fries

A lanky, forlorn crisp, torn by existential angst as it tries, unsuccessfully, to steer a middle way between the extremes of full-fat chip, with all the ritual that entails, and the pure, Reformed crisp that has left it all behind.

✠ ✠ ✠

Charles Longley – Hula Hoops

Yay! Hula Hoops! Open a pack, invite some mates round. Heck, invite every bishop in the Anglican Communion round. Two hours later: they're absolutely binned, shouting at each other about who should be the next Bishop of Zululand while they crush Hula Hoops underfoot.

✠ ✠ ✠

John Bird Sumner – Sunbites

A crisp engaged in a frantic PR exercise to convince people that it is not, in fact, a crisp. 'Look, look! I'm cooked in healthy oil, I'm pro Catholic emancipation, I'm iffy on infant baptism, AND I'm multigrain!' Get over it, mate. You're a crisp.

✠ ✠ ✠

William Howley – Wheat Crunchies

A crisp determined to deny that modernity is happening. It sits on its corner shop shelf, draped in purple, denying the advent of the potato as the primary base for bagged snacks, and voting against political reform at every opportunity.

✠ ✠ ✠

APPENDIX

Charles Manners-Sutton – Kettle Chips

The sort of crisp that would have the Duke of Rutland for an uncle.

John Moore – Roast Beef Monster Munch

A bold, beefy crisp. The kind of crisp that would 'dispense patronage with somewhat more than due regard to the interests of his own family', and there'd be nothing you could do about it.

Frederick Cornwallis – Tyrrell's Lightly Sea Salted

Competent but uninspiring. No one's favourite crisp is Tyrrell's Lightly Sea Salted; no one's favourite Archbishop of Canterbury is Frederick Cornwallis.

Thomas Secker – Transform-a-Snack

The ultimate in flexible, politically adaptable corner shop fare. Is it Anglican or is it a Dissenter? Is it a chip stick or an onion ring? Is it for George II or the Prince of Wales? It's all of them! It's Transform-a-Snack!

Matthew Hutton – Salt & Shake

Just as Matthew Hutton fell, by dying, at the first hurdle in the role of Archbishop of Canterbury, so Salt & Shake, by making you apply your own seasoning, falls at the first hurdle in the role of being a convenient on-the-go potato snack.

✠ ✠ ✠

Thomas Herring – Worcester Sauce Walkers

Can you explain to a foreigner why these crisps are a good thing? No. Would you want these crisps on your side, whipping up public support, during the Jacobite rebellion? Yes.

✠ ✠ ✠

John Potter – Quavers

A light crisp; an ethereal crisp. The sort of crisp that would translate Plutarch in its teens and be an Oxford professor in its twenties. But is it the kind of crisp to be relied on to restore the Convocation of Canterbury? Alas, it is not that crisp.

✠ ✠ ✠

APPENDIX

John Tillotson – Ritz Crisp & Thin

It never wanted to be a crisp; it was happy in amongst the cracker aisle. And then BANG – Glorious Revolution happens, and next thing it knows it's in the House of Lords, sitting next to some Roasted Chicken and Thyme Sensations.

William Sancroft – Squares

Squares don't care what your preformed conceptions about crisps are: they took an oath to sit in the crisp section of the supermarket and so sit in the crisp section is what they'll do. You take your Williamite allegiance/round-shaping elsewhere.

Gilbert Sheldon – Flamin' Hot Monster Munch

When you've got such an eye for ladies that even Samuel Pepys says you're a 'very wencher', there's only one crisp you can be. Fetch a fire extinguisher and rename Oxford's main university building the Flamin' Hot Arena, it's Big G Sheldon.

William Juxon – Roast Chicken Walkers

Imagine you're Charles I's mum packing his lunch box for the day he gets his head cut off – what crisps would you put in to give him a bit of comfort as he goes through martyrdom on the scaffold? Roast Chicken, obviously.

✠ ✠ ✠

William Laud – Pickled Onion Monster Munch

I fancy something different with my meal deal today, you say to yourself in Sainos, and pick out these. Next thing you know, all your altars are back at the east end, your fingers smell oniony, and your Scottish Prayer Book's been revised.

✠ ✠ ✠

George Abbot – Chipsticks

A crisp that seems to know what it's about. However, this is not a crisp you can rely on. If there is one crisp that'll let you down by turning into maizey, bitter mush in your mouth or shooting a gamekeeper on a hunting trip, it's this crisp.

✠ ✠ ✠

Appendix

Richard Bancroft – Roasted Chicken and Thyme
Sensations

They look down with a weary condescension on the excesses of their fellow crisps. They're the crisps that would go out of their way to extinguish 'all that fire in England which had been kindled at Geneva'.

John Whitgift – Scampi Fries

A crisp that knows how to make an entrance. Whether turning up to their cathedral city with a retinue of eight hundred horses or stinking out an entire pub with their weird fishy aroma, there's no underestimating this bad boy.

Edmund Grindal – Space Raiders

An objectively disappointing crisp. 'Ooh,' you think to yourself, 'I bet that crisp packs a delicious flavour punch and could sort out Puritan excesses once and for all. And all for 20p!' Wrong. On both counts. You get what you pay for.

Matthew Parker – Burts Guinness Crisps

The sort of crisp that would have a malicious rumour started that it was actually consecrated to episcopal orders in the back room of a pub.

✢ ✢ ✢

Reginald, Cardinal Pole – Doritos Chilli Heatwave

A crisp with obvious Spanish influences; keen on dialling up the temperature, especially if you're a Protestant.

✢ ✢ ✢

Thomas Cranmer – Ready Salted Walkers.

Big Daddy crisp. The Crispfather. The crisp that has shaped our culture and language more than we will ever know, helping to make all the other delicious savoury snacks possible.

✢ ✢ ✢

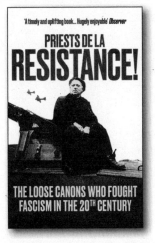

'A timely and uplifting book... Hugely enjoyable' *Observer*

PRIESTS DE LA RESISTANCE!

THE LOOSE CANONS WHO FOUGHT FASCISM IN THE 20TH CENTURY

Whoever said that Christians had to be meek and mild hadn't met Father Kir – parish priest and French resistance hero ... and immortalised every time Kir Royale is drunk. And they probably weren't thinking of Archbishop Damaskinos who, threatened with the firing squad by the Germans, replied, 'Please respect our traditions – in Greece we *hang* our Archbishops.'

Wherever fascism has taken root, it has met with resistance. From taking a bullet for a frightened schoolgirl in Alabama to riding on the bonnet of a tank during the liberation of France, each of the hard-drinking, chain-smoking clerics featured in *Priests de la Résistance* were willing to give their lives for a world they believed in – even as their superiors beckoned them to safety.

In this spellbinding new collection, the Reverend Fergus Butler-Gallie, bestselling author of A *Field Guide to the English Clergy*, presents fifteen men and women who dared to stand up to fascism, proving that some hearts will never be conquered.